OSPREY COMBAT AIRCRAFT • 56

US MARINE CORPS AND RAAF HORNET UNITS OF OPERATION *IRAQI FREEDOM*

SERIES EDITOR: TONY HOLMES

OSPREY COMBAT AIRCRAFT • 56

US MARINE CORPS AND RAAF HORNET UNITS OF OPERATION *IRAQI FREEDOM*

TONY HOLMES

OSPREY
PUBLISHING

Front cover
On 13 April 2003, lone VMFA(AW)-533 F/A-18D BuNo 164959, alias 'Akimbo 34', headed for Tikrit in search of targets. Strapped into the cockpit was FAC(A)-qualified crew Maj 'Sack' Rowell (pilot) and Capt 'Oedi' Glover, both of whom had seen considerable combat in the previous 24 days. As FAC(A)s, they had been in high demand, operating all over Iraq controlling the battlefield for TACAIR assets, as well as calling in mortar, artillery and attack helicopter fires. The FAC(A) crew would act as a communications relay, as well as the primary targeting source, running in to mark targets with rockets, or identifying aim points and securing bomb coordinates that allowed targets to be attacked expeditiously, and accurately. Collateral damage and positive ID issues ultimately rested with the FAC(A) crew too.

'Akimbo 34's' experiences in the early afternoon of 13 April were typical of those encountered by FAC(A) crews throughout OIF. Due to their paucity in number, the FAC(A) jets would usually sortie by themselves and remain on-station for hours on end thanks to their status as 'priority one gas-getters' with the 'big wing' tankers on station. On this day, 'Akimbo 34' single-handedly took charge of the airspace overhead several airfields to the east of Tikrit in which TACAIR assets were operating. Arriving on-station at noon, and remaining on call until 1530 hrs thanks to several visits to nearby tanker tracks, Rowell and Glover provided targeting control for USAF F-16CJs and A-10s, Marine Corps AV-8Bs and RAF Tornado GR 4s during the mission.

At this late stage in the war CENTCOM was worried about leadership targets escaping to nearby Iran in aircraft that had been kept serviceable at these sites. It had also received reports that SOF teams had seen drums being buried near Al Sahra airfield. Coalition Intelligence suggested that these may contain chemicals that could be spread via helicopter or aircraft. The latter, therefore, were priority targets.

Overflying Al Sahra, which was defended by two SA-2 SAM sites, 'Akimbo 34' identified numerous light aircraft, including multiple L-29 Delfins, L-39 Albatros and S260s.

First published in Great Britain in 2006 by Osprey Publishing
Midland House, West Way, Botley, Oxford, OX2 0PH
443 Park Avenue South, New York, NY 10016, USA

ISBN 1 84176 847 2

Page design by Tony Truscott
Cover Artwork by Mark Postlethwaite
Aircraft Profiles by Chris Davey
Index by Alan Thatcher
Originated by United Graphics, Singapore
Printed and bound in China through Bookbuilders

06 07 08 09 10   10 09 08 07 06 05 04 03 02 01

For a catalogue of all books published by Osprey please contact:
NORTH AMERICA
Osprey Direct, C/o Random House Distribution Center,
400 Hahn Road, Westminster, MD 21157
E-mail:info@ospreydirect.com

ALL OTHER REGIONS
Osprey Direct UK, P.O. Box 140 Wellingborough, Northants, NN8 2FA, UK
E-mail: info@ospreydirect.co.uk
www.ospreypublishing.com

EDITOR'S NOTE
To make this series as authoritative as possible, the Editor would be interested in hearing from any individual with relevant OIF I/II photographs, documentation or first-hand experiences. Please contact Tony Holmes via e-mail at: tony.holmes@osprey-jets.freeserve.co.uk or tonyholmes67@yahoo.co.uk

Dedication
This volume is dedicated to the memories of Maj John C Spahr and his wingman, Capt Kelly C Hinz, both from VMFA-323, who lost their lives in a mid-air collision over Iraq in bad weather on the night of 2 May 2005

They were granted approval to engage these targets, and duly hit them with a GBU-16 LGB and an AGM-65E LMAV. A strafing run was also made on an L-39 shortly after the LMAV had destroyed the first Albatros targeted by 'Akimbo 34'. Replacement VMFA(AW)-533 FAC(A) crew 'Akimbo 35' arrived on-station shortly after the gunnery pass, and they too attacked aircraft scattered around the airfield. Having quickly briefed the in-bound F/A-18D crew on remaining targets in the area, 'Akimbo 34' returned to base (*Cover artwork by Mark Postlethwaite*)

CONTENTS

INTRODUCTION

Some 84 of the 250 Hornets committed by Central Command to Operation *Iraqi Freedom* (OIF) proudly bore MARINE titling on their rear fuselages. A further 14 were marked with the distinctive kangaroo roundel of the Royal Australian Air Force (RAAF). The exploits achieved by the units that flew these jets into combat are detailed in this volume, the third of three titles that I have written on what has been dubbed by many TACAIR insiders the 'Hornet's War'. Although the bulk of this book deals with the major hostilities phase of OIF I, which ran from 20 March to 20 April 2003, the decade of pre-war OSW missions and ongoing post-war OIF II operations are also covered in significant detail.

Acknowledgements

A significant number of Marine Corps pilots and Weapons Systems Officers who flew the Hornet into combat in OIF I/II have made a contribution to this book, and the finished volume is considerably better for their valued input. Access to the men and women of the US armed forces who are currently engaged in the War on Terror has tightened up considerably in the post-9/11 world that we now live in. However, thanks to the personnel who man the Public Affairs Division of the Headquarters Marine Corps in the Pentagon, I was able to meet and interview key Hornet aircrew soon after their return home from OIF. I would like to take this opportunity to thank Capt Shawn Turner, who handled my initial request so expeditiously, and Maj Robert Premo, Aviation Systems Weapons Requirement Branch, who fielded my initial request for access.

As usual, my old friend Cdr Peter Mersky was relied upon to provide constructive criticism of the text. I also owe a great debt to Maj Doug Glover, formerly of VMFA(AW)-533 and now with MAWTS-1, who got the ball rolling by vouching for me with many of his OIF colleagues from MAG-11. He also read through the manuscript to ensure its accuracy from an end-user's perspective. Lt Col Mike Burt, Majs Charles Dockery, Jeff Ertwine, Brian Foster, Eric Jakubowski and Marvin Reed and Capts Ed Bahret, Matthew Brown, Christopher Holloway, Matt Merrill and Guy Ravey also performed this vital task – thanks to one and all. Timely information/photos were provided by Capt Jan Jacobs of Tailhook, Capt Zip Rausa of ANA, Lt Col Doug Steele, Dan Meador, David Isby, Erik Hildebrandt, Richard Siudak and Bob Sanchez.

Finally, thanks to the pilots from the following units, whose experiences and photographs fill this volume;

MAG-11 – Lt Col Doug Pasnik (2002-03) and Maj Mike McGinn
VMFA-115 – Capt Eric Jakubowski (2002-03) and Capt Chris Holloway (2003-05)
VMFA(AW)-121 – Maj Jeff Ertwine and Capt Charles Dockery
VMFA(AW)-224 – Capt Matthew Brown
VMFA(AW)-225 – Capt Ed Bahret
VMFA-232 – Lt Cols Mike Burt and Doug Kurth, Majs Brian Foster (OIF FAC) and Eric Jakubowski (2004-05) and Capts Garret Rampulla, Heath Reed, Justin Knox and Byron Sullivan
VMFA(AW)-242 – Lt Col Doug Pasnik (2004-05), Maj Marvin Reed and Capt Matt Merrill
VMFA-323 – Capt Robert Peterson (2002-05) and Capt Guy Ravey (2002-05)
VMFA(AW)-533 – Capt Doug Glover

I have also received considerable assistance from a number of individuals in Australia who have aided my efforts to chronicle the exploits of the RAAF's No 75 Sqn in Operation *Falconer*. I would like to thank Maj Waylan Cain (US Marine Corps Hornet exchange officer), Sqn Ldrs Ken Bowes and Simon Branch, Flt Lts Peter Weekes (No 75 Sqn) and James Atkinson (current RAAF Hornet exchange officer with the US Navy), Tony Holmes Snr and Mike Mirkovic for their help.

Tony Holmes, Sevenoaks, Kent, November 2005

BUILD-UP TO WAR

For the first time since Operation *Desert Storm* in 1991, the US Marine Corps sent a complete Marine Aircraft Group (MAG) into the field as part of the Coalition build for OIF. As with *Desert Storm*, when the backbone of the Bahrain-based MAG-11 was provided by seven Hornet units, the Marine Corps' primary TACAIR asset in OIF was once again the venerable F/A-18. Two C- and three D-model units called Al Jaber, in northern Kuwait, home for the duration of the 2003 conflict, and again they were controlled by MAG-11.

In the intervening 12 years from *Desert Storm* to OIF, Marine Hornet units had very occasionally operated in the area with Central Command (CENTCOM) as part of the United Nations' mandated Operation *Southern Watch* (OSW). The latter, established in August 1992, had grown out of Operation *Provide Comfort*, which had seen the enforcement of a No-Fly Zone in northern Iraq in the wake of *Desert Storm*. The No-Fly Zone had been established by Coalition air forces in an effort to offer protection to the Kurdish population in the north from Saddam's forces. Initially established over all Iraqi territory north of the 36th parallel as part of *Provide Comfort* in late 1991, the legality of this mission was mandated by UN Security Council Resolution 688.

When Shi'ite Muslims also began to suffer persecution in the south, a No-Fly Zone was created with UN backing in southern Iraq as Operation *Southern Watch* (OSW) on 26 August 1992. Joint Task Force-Southwest Asia (JTF-SWA), consisting of units from the US, Britain, France and Saudi Arabia, stood up on the same date to oversee the running of OSW.

Like the operation in the north, which was officially titled Operation *Northern Watch* (ONW) on 1 January 1997, OSW saw US, British and French aircraft enforcing the Security Council mandate that prevented the Iraq Air Force (IrAF) from flying military aircraft or helicopters below the 32nd parallel – this was increased to the 33rd parallel in September 1996. Further restrictions, including the introduction of a No-Drive Zone in the south following Iraq's mobilisation and deployment of forces along the Kuwait border in October 1994, were introduced several years later to stop surface-to-air missile (SAM) launchers being moved south.

During the decade that OSW was conducted, one of the major participants in its enforcement was the US Navy. A seemingly endless series of carrier battle/task groups, controlled by Fifth Fleet (which had been formed in July 1995) as part of the unified

Armed with a single AGM-88C HARM beneath each wing, VMFA-251's F/A-18C 'TBolt 210' (BuNo 164891) closes on the deck of USS *John F Kennedy* (CV-67) at the end of a SEAD sortie in the 'Box' in early 2000. Assigned to CVW-1, the unit completed three OSW deployments between 1995 and 2000, followed by an OEF combat cruise in 2001-02. The Millennium deployment of 1999-2000 was an eventful one for VMFA-251, as CO Lt Col Doug Yurovich told the author in February 2000;

'We have had a chance to use all of the ordnance available to us in combat on this deployment, bar our air-to-air missiles and our 20 mm cannon – we have practised some 60-degree strafing on point targets on the Udairi range in Kuwait, but my admiral is not overly keen on us firing our cannon for real against targets in Iraq! The squadron has employed a whole generation of weapons on this cruise from laser Maverick, which is very old, to JDAM. I am pretty sure that we are the first Marine unit to drop JDAM in combat. This happened in early February 2000 – we have proven our proficiency with both this weapon and JDAM, despite possessing only two GPS-capable Hornets. The unit also performed CVW-1's only successful LMAV shot on cruise, and we have had good GBU-12 and GBU-16 LGB drops too' (*US Navy*)

CENTCOM, oversaw operations in the region. Typically, an aircraft carrier would be on station in the Northern Arabian Gulf (NAG) at all times, vessels spending around three to four months of a standard six-month deployment committed to OSW. Ships from both the Atlantic and Pacific fleets took it in turns to 'stand the watch', sharing the policing duties in the No-Fly Zone with USAF and RAF assets ashore at bases in Saudi Arabia, Kuwait, Oman and other allied countries in the region.

Although most units committed to OSW from carriers steaming in the NAG bore NAVY titling on their tactical grey fuselages, occasionally Marine Corps Hornets would arrive on station as part of a carrier air wing – the Marine Corps began permanent fleet integration with four of its single-seat F/A-18C units post-*Desert Storm*. Flying identical missions to the other ship-based light strike units, VMFA-251, 312, 314 and 323 all gained combat experience over southern Iraq during a series of cruises with CVW-1, 3, 9 and 2, respectively, between 1995 and 2003.

OSW's original brief was to deter the repression of the Kurdish and Shi'ite populations and impose a No-Fly Zone, but it soon became obvious to the Coalition that the Iraqi Army was more than capable of dealing with the disruptive elements in both the north and the south without having to involve the IrAF. Frustrated by its inability to defend the people it had encouraged to rise up and overthrow Saddam's regime in 1991, the US-led Coalition subtly changed the emphasis of its ONW and OSW mission. This saw the systematic monitoring of Iraqi military activity in the area evolve from being a useful secondary mission tasking to the primary role of the crews conducting these sorties from the mid 1990s. By December 1998, the justification put forward by the US government for the continuation of both ONW and OSW was the protection of Iraq's neighbours from any potential aggression, and to ensure the admission, and safety, of UN weapons inspectors.

Most OSW missions were mundane and boring according to the aircrew involved. However, this all changed with the implementation of Operation *Desert Fox* on 16 December 1998, which saw the launching of a four-day aerial offensive ostensibly aimed at curbing Iraq's ability to produce Weapons of Mass Destruction (WMD). Although triggered by Saddam's unwillingness to cooperate with UN inspections of weapons sites, many observers believed that the primary aim of *Desert Fox* was to attack the Iraqi leadership in a series of decapitation strikes. To this end, a presidential palace south of Baghdad was hit, as were buildings housing the Special Security Organisation and the Special Republican Guard.

The aircraft carriers USS *Enterprise* (CVN-65) and USS *Carl Vinson* (CVN-70) played a key role in *Desert Fox*, the vessels' CVW-3 and CVW-11 flying more than 400 sorties in the 25+ strikes launched during the campaign. In the vanguard of the missions flown from CVN-65 was VMFA-312, which dropped laser-guided bombs and launched AGM-88 High-speed Anti-Radiation Missiles (HARM). The unit also became the first Marine Corps squadron to employ the AGM-154 Joint Stand Off Weapon (JSOW) during the course of this deployment, which also saw VMFA-312 involved in Operation *Allied Force* in the Balkans.

Although *Desert Fox* lasted for just four days, its consequences were felt right up until OIF in March 2003. Proclaiming a victory after UN weapons inspectors had left Iraq on the eve of the bombing campaign,

Saddam now brazenly challenged patrolling ONW and OSW jets by moving mobile SAM batteries and AAA weapons into the exclusion zones. Both were used with increasing frequency in the coming months, and IrAF jets also started to push more regularly into the No-Fly Zones.

In the post-*Desert Fox* world, these violations provoked a swift, but measured, response from JTF-SWA's Combined Air Operations Center (CAOC), which controlled the entire No-Fly Zone mission planning element, and created a daily Air Tasking Order (ATO) for all Coalition participants (both naval and shore-based aviation assets). Typically, such missions were devised within the CAOC-approved pre-planned retaliatory strike framework, and they soon became known as Response Options (ROs). The latter allowed No-Fly Zone enforcers to react to threats or incursions in a coordinated manner through the execution of agreed ROs against pre-determined targets such as SAM and AAA sites and command and control nodes.

Following VMFA-312's departure from the NAG at the end of *Desert Fox*, the next Marine unit to see action in southern Iraq was VMFA-323. Assigned to CVW-2 in 1993, and a veteran of two previous OSW cruises with the air wing aboard USS *Constellation* (CV-64), VMFA-323 dropped more than 16,000 lbs of ordnance on military targets as it executed ROs between July and November 1999.

VMFA-251, embarked in USS *John F Kennedy* (CV-67) with CVW-1, replaced VMFA-323 and CVW-2 in late 1999, and it also expended bombs and missiles in anger during four months of OSW patrols. From March to May 2000, CVW-9, assigned to USS *John C Stennis* (CVN-74), undertook the OSW mission. Amongst its trio of Hornet units was VMFA-314, conducting its second cruise with the air wing. Deployment highlights were summarised in the following report by the unit's Capt Mark Christenson, run in the Fall 2000 issue of *Hook* magazine;

'"Black Knight" pilots delivered several LGBs and the new GBU-31 JDAM on Iraqi military targets. While the OSW missions did not come as frequently as in past years, the flights proved more exciting as each visit to Iraq had the potential to become a rapid-response air strike. On several occasions, VMFA-314 pilots, along with other CVW-9 crews, responded to conduct real-time targeting of Iraqi military targets as directed by JTF-SWA. Using precision weapons, direct hits were later confirmed after "Black Knight" pilots dropped their ordnance, and they were credited with the destruction of Iraqi surface-to-air defence sites.'

The level of conflict in the southern region remained high into the new millennium, and between March 2000 and March 2001, Coalition aircraft were engaged more than 500 times by SAMs and AAA while flying 10,000 sorties into Iraqi airspace. In response to this aggression, which had seen Coalition jets fired on 60 times since 1 January 2001, US and British strike aircraft dropped bombs on 38 occasions. The most comprehensive of these RO strikes – the biggest since *Desert Fox* – occurred on 16 February 2001 when CVW-3 (again including VMFA-312 within its number), operating from USS *Harry S Truman* (CVN-75), hit five command, control and communications sites.

CVN-75 was replaced on-station in the NAG by CV-64 in late April 2001, and once again VMFA-323 commenced flying OSW missions with CVW-2 – the unit's fourth such deployment in six years. Although

occasionally seeing AAA, the squadron's four months in the NAG were remarkably quiet.

Things would be significantly different the next time CVW-2 and VMFA-323 arrived on station in the NAG in December 2002 as a direct result of the most devastating single act of terrorism the world has ever seen. On the morning of 11 September 2001, just four days prior to CV-64 finishing its six-month deployment and pulling back into its homeport of North Island, California, al-Qaeda flew two hijacked airliners into the World Trade Center, in New York City, and a single jet into the Pentagon. The subsequent declaration of the War on Terror by President George W Bush saw US carrier battle groups under Fifth Fleet control immediately removed from their OSW station and pushed further east into the Arabian Sea and Indian Ocean in order to support Operation *Enduring Freedom* (OEF) in Afghanistan.

With the bulk of the tactical air power in this conflict provided by carrier aircraft flying arduous eight- to ten-hour missions over land-locked Afghanistan, OSW No-Fly Zone operations by the US Navy would be halted for the first time in almost a decade.

OSW MISSIONS ASHORE

Although the vast majority of OSW missions flown by Marine Corps Hornets were undertaken by units flying carrier-based single-seat F/A-18Cs, in March 2000 F/A-18D-equipped VMFA(AW)-121 returned to the theatre for the first time since *Desert Storm*. One of the aircrew to participate in this unique deployment was Weapons System Officer (WSO) Capt Charles Dockery, who told the author;

'We were in-country from March through to June. We flew all of our missions from Al Jaber, in Kuwait, having come into theatre to replace an Air Force A-10 unit. We were co-located with an Air Force F-16 squadron, so the whole set up of the operation was primarily USAF-driven. We were viewed by the CAOC as essentially A-10 replacements, but with a lot more capability to boot.

'The unit was initially sent into Kuwait to simply perform the A-10's Combat Search And Rescue (CSAR) mission, but we also arrived with JSOW and JDAM capability, which was then very new in OSW. Indeed, the F-15Es and F-16s were not J-weapon capable at the time, meaning that the CAOC could only employ GPS-guided weapons when there was an aircraft carrier on-station in the NAG. We were able to fill in the gap when there was no task group in the area. Therefore, although we

When CVW-1/CV-67 departed the NAG on 1 March 2000, their place on-station in the NAG was taken by CVW-9 and USS *John C Stennis* (CVN-74). A third of the 36-strong Hornet force embarked in the vessel was provided by VMFA-314, which had been the very first Marine Corps light strike unit to participate in OSW when it arrived in the NAG with CVW-11 aboard USS *Abraham Lincoln* (CVN-72) in August 1992. Transitioning from F/A-18As to new Lot XVIII F/A-18Cs in 1996, VMFA-314 was assigned to CVW-9 the following year and subsequently completed two OSW cruises (in 1997 and 2000), a single OEF combat deployment (in 2001-02) and the 2003 *WestPac* cruise with the air wing, before reverting back to MAG-11 control. This photograph of Lot XVII jet 'Knight 203' (BuNo 164956) in afterburner on bow catapult one was taken in April 2000. This aircraft is almost certainly heading for the Udairi bombing range in Kuwait, as it is armed with an unguided 1000-lb Mk 83 general purpose bomb, fitted with a metallic blue M904E4 fuse in the nose. Only precision-guided ordnance was cleared for use in the 'Box' by the CAOC (*US Navy*)

Right
The 1000-lb GBU-16B/B was the stock RO weapon of choice in OSW until the first JDAM arrived in-theatre in late 1999. Flying some of the first J-weapon-capable jets assigned to CENTCOM, VMFA(AW)-121 nevertheless dropped a handful of LGBs during its three months at Al Jaber (*VMFA(AW)-121*)

primarily performed the CSAR role, we also tacked on the J-weapon precision bombing mission whenever we ventured into Iraq.

'Things were pretty quiet during the period we were in-theatre, all the action having taken place in 1999 and then again in early 2001! Nevertheless, my unit flew a lot more OSW missions than the Marine Corps Hornet squadrons that followed us in 2001-02. We employed a fair number of JDAM, JSOW and LGBs, but not a lot of HARM. These missions were standard OSW fare, where you trolled around and sometimes you got shot at, and other times you didn't. Occasionally you would be given permission to retaliate with a bomb, but most of the time you returned to base with your ordnance still on the jet.'

The next Marine Corps unit to deploy to Al Jaber as stand ins for the CSAR mission was VMFA(AW)-225, which arrived in-theatre in 2001. Amongst the WSOs deployed was Capt Ed Bahret, who recalled;

'We were sent to Kuwait rather than heading to Turkey or Italy, as was usually the case then. We dropped two JDAM on cable repeater stations during our time in-theatre, and that was it. Although this deployment was uneventful in the main, it did mean that most of us in the unit were familiar with how things were run by the CAOC in OSW prior to our arrival in Kuwait for OIF.'

The last Marine units committed to OSW were VMFA(AW)-332 and VMFA-212, which sent a composite detachment of six F/A-18Ds and six F/A-18Cs to Al Jaber from their forward-deployed base at Iwakuni, in Japan, in April 2002. Both squadrons then rotated crews through the Kuwait detachment from their home base. This was the first, and only, time that such a deployment was handled this way.

In March 2000 VMFA(AW)-121 made OSW history by becoming the first land-based Marine Corps Hornet unit to be assigned to CENTCOM. Remaining in-theatre for three months, and operating from Al Jaber, in Kuwait, the unit performed a total of 287 sorties into southern Iraq. JDAM, JSOW, LGBs and HARM were all used by VMFA(AW)-121 in anger against radar and AAA sites in Ar Rumaylah, Al Kut, Basra, As Samawah, Qalat Sukkar, Al Numinayah, Ash Shatrah and As Samawah. Armed with AIM-7Ms, AIM-120Cs and AIM-9Ms, this VMFA(AW)-121 section are conducting a DCA CAP over Iraq (*VMFA(AW)-121*)

CARRIERS RETURN

By the spring of 2002, the Taliban regime had been removed from

power in Afghanistan, and the US government's focus of attention returned once again to its old foe in the region, Saddam Hussein. Proof of this came with the arrival of USS *George Washington* (CVN-73) and its embarked CVW-17 in the NAG in late August 2002, the vessel's subsequent assignment to OSW marking the first time that a carrier task group had performed this mission in a year. Within days of its arrival on station, the air wing was conducting RO strikes after being consistently engaged by AAA and SAM radars during patrols over southern Iraq.

While the tactical jets of CVW-17 continued to perform OSW missions, in Washington, D.C. the case for war against Iraq was gaining momentum as discussions about the country's alleged development and stockpiling of weapons of mass destruction (WMD) reached fever pitch. Links between Saddam's regime and Osama Bin Laden's al-Qaeda terrorist network were also played up by the Bush administration, and the end product of all this talk was the decision, in September 2002, by US Defence Secretary Donald Rumsfeld to step up the level of response to Iraqi threats to US and British aircraft conducting OSW missions.

The adoption of ROs as the primary means of enforcing OSW had evolved to match the Coalition's desire to ensure the safety of its aircrew flying over Iraq. Initially, the near-immediate air strike response to SAFIREs (surface-to-air fires, involving AAA or SAMs) that had been the norm before and immediately after *Desert Fox* was replaced with delayed, punitive strikes that were usually flown on the same day as the No-Fly Zone violation had taken place. This RO evolved post-9/11 into an even more considered approach, whereby the Coalition adopted the policy of attacking any military target in the southern No-Fly Zone. It did not even have to be the one that prompted the reaction in the first place. This, in turn, led to the adoption of pre-planned RO methodology in late 2002.

The first Marine Corps unit to feel the effects of the more aggressive stance being taken by the Coalition in respect to Iraqi OSW violations was VMFA-323, which arrived in the NAG with CV-64 on 17 December 2002 to start its fifth such deployment as part of CVW-2. Both 'Connie' and its air wing were seasoned OSW campaigners, having enforced the No-Fly Zone on their previous four cruises between 1995 and 2001. In that time CVW-2 had racked up an impressive 50 weeks of OSW flying, its units having flown in excess of 5000 sorties policing the No-Fly Zone. For a full description of a typical OSW mission see *Osprey Combat Aircraft 46 – US Navy Hornet Squadrons of Operation Iraqi Freedom Part One*.

The air wing undertook its first mission into Iraq on 19 December 2002, and F/A-18Cs struck targets as part of an RO the following day. Commenting on this first air wing strike, CVW-2's commanding officer, Capt Mark Fox, remarked;

On 20 December 2002, a division of VMFA-323 F/A-18Cs became CVW-2's first bomb droppers on what would prove to be an historic final cruise aboard CV-64. The CENTCOM press release for the action read, in part, as follows;

'In response to Iraqi acts against Coalition aircraft monitoring compliance of United Nations Security Council Resolutions over Southern Iraq, Operation *Southern Watch* Coalition aircraft used precision-guided weapons today to target two Iraqi air defence communication facilities. The sites were located near An Nasiriyah and Basra, in southern Iraq. The strikes occurred at approximately 0230 hrs EST.'

Four 1000-lb GBU-35s were dropped, these being the first of 23 JDAM expended by the unit during OSW – a further 52 PDU-5/B Psychological Dispersal Units (each packed with 15,000 leaflets) were also released by VMFA-323 over southern Iraq in the lead up to OIF. The four pilots involved in the 20 December RO strike are seen here posing with squadron armourers on the flightdeck of CV-64 soon after returning from the mission (*VMFA-323*)

'It immediately became clear that we would not repeat the 2001 deployment's "Groundhog Day" pattern. Conducting an RO attack on only our second day of operations in the NAG, we had destroyed several different Iraqi targets and delivered more ordnance and hit more aim points in that one strike than we had during the entire 2001 deployment.'

VMFA-323 played a major part in CVW-2's endless cycle of OSW missions in the lead up to OIF, being the only sea-based Marine Corps Hornet unit in the NAG. One of the pilots writing up 'green ink' sorties (combat missions) in his logbook was first-tour 'nugget' Capt Guy Ravey;

'By the time VMFA-323 went on deployment with CVW-2 in late 2002, the unit had been cruising with the air wing for eight years straight. This meant that we were very well integrated into CVW-2's overall warfighting strategy. We were, in effect, just another strike fighter squadron, but manned by Marines. The unit had firmly established a reputation for itself as a fully functioning partner within the CVW-2 team. This meant that there were no problems with a Marine leading a mission that also involved Navy elements within the force make-up.

'We showed up in the NAG on 17 December, which was the perfect time for us, as it allowed even the new guys like myself to get comfortable with flying operationally in the area and to figure out how to employ weapons effectively in combat. As part of the preparation for war, we made regular use of the massive Udairi bombing range in Kuwait. I got to drop a number of dumb bombs on targets here, and also worked closely with Army and Marine Forward Air Controllers (FACs).

'We also tested the effectiveness of marking devices that had been newly applied to Coalition vehicles just prior to the war kicking off in an attempt to reduce "blue-on-blue" incidents. These took the form of IR stripes that we could read through our FLIR.

'Our solid reputation within CVW-2 for getting the job done, combined with more than a little luck, resulted in us getting more ROs during OSW than either of our sister light strike squadrons in CVW-2, VFA-137 and VFA-151. Around 90 per cent of the ROs that we flew were against cable repeater stations lining the roads from Baghdad to Basra. Although these targets were not overly satisfying to hit from a warfighter's perspective, they were politically neutral as there was no fear that you would accidentally kill Iraqi civilians – the stations targeted were situated in open desert. We dropped nothing but JDAM in OSW.

'As we got closer to OIF, we started to hit other targets in RO strikes too, such as radio relay sites and artillery along the Iraq/Kuwait border. There was a conscious effort made by the CAOC to target command and control and Baath party buildings in the final days of OSW. In response, the Iraqis fired more AAA in defence of these targets, although this was usually only two or three S-60s firing multiple rounds, rather than the odd shot that occasionally took us by surprise earlier in the cruise.'

As Capt Ravey recalled, the only ordnance dropped by VMFA-323 in OSW was the GPS-guided JDAM, which was undoubtedly the CAOC's weapon of choice post-OEF thanks to it being wholly autonomous after release, unlike laser-guided or electro-optical munitions whose accuracy can be affected by bad weather or poor targeting solutions. A clinically accurate weapon against fixed targets, which proliferated in OSW, JDAM is effectively a standard Mk 83 (1000-lb), Mk 84 (2000-lb) or

A VMFA-323 F/A-18C tops off its tanks from a USAF KC-10 mid way through an OSW patrol in early 2003. The aircraft carries a single GBU-35, as well as two AIM-9Ms and an AIM-120C. The jet's external fuel tanks are mounted in 'double bubble' configuration, which means that one wing has both pylons free for ordnance. This is known as the 'hard wing' configuration, and all Hornet units adopted this layout in OIF. Jets venturing into the 'Box' pre-OIF carried air-to-air missiles in case the IrAF headed south. VMFA-323's Capt Guy Ravey explained;

'Throughout this time the IrAF was continuing to fly on a daily basis, but above the No-Fly Zone. The Iraqi command and control network monitored our packages in the "Box", waiting for us to leave, and once we had departed, it would order jets to conduct a high-speed pass 20 miles south of the 32nd parallel. By the time we got more aircraft on-station, the IrAF machines had long since returned to their bases. I was airborne in the "Box" on one occasion when a MiG-23 was detected on radar by an orbiting AWACS, but the fighter was legitimately flying in Iraqi airspace, so there was nothing I could do about it. Although he had been designated as a bandit by the AWACS controller, he had not been declared hostile, so I could not uncage my missiles and shoot him down' (*VMFA-323*)

BLU-109 (2000-lb penetrator) unguided bomb fitted with a GPS guidance control unit (GCU), mid-body ventral strakes and a tail unit that has steerable control fins.

Developed by precision weapons pioneer Boeing in the late 1990s, JDAM differs from other GPS-guided weapons (AGM-130 and EGBU-15) in that it guides autonomously after release – it cannot be steered or fed updated targeting data once dropped. The 'baseline' JDAM is considered to be a 'near precision' weapon, its GCU relying on a three-axis Inertial Navigation System (INS) and a GPS receiver to provide its pre-planned or in-flight targeting capability. The INS is a back-up system should the GPS lose satellite reception or be jammed.

With GPS guidance at its heart, the JDAM can only be employed by an aircraft fitted with an on-board GPS system so that GPS-computed coordinates can be downloaded to the weapon for both the target itself and the weapon release point. That way the jet's onboard INS remains as accurate as possible while the weapon is acquiring a GPS signal after being released. This effectively means that the jet has to have a MIL-STD 1760 data bus and compatible pylon wiring in order to programme the bomb's aim point, intended trajectory shape and impact geometry.

All this information will have been loaded by the pilot onto his MU (Memory Unit, fitted into the F/A-18C/D) or MDL (Mission Data Loader, fitted into the F/A-18A+) via the TAMPS (Tactical Aircrew Mission Planning System) pre-flight, should the Hornet be going after a fixed target. If, however, a target of opportunity crops up after launch, the pilot simply has to enter its coordinates into the Hornet's mission computer and the bomb's aim point is automatically altered.

Achieving initial operational capability in 1997, JDAM made its frontline debut during the NATO-led bombing campaign in Serbia and Kosovo during Operation *Allied Force* in 1999. It was then progressively employed during OSW primarily by the US Navy, until the weapon really began to capture headlines during OEF thanks to the exploits of Navy Hornet units operating from carriers assigned to the conflict.

As in OSW and then OEF, OIF saw Navy and Marine Corps strike units uploading known grid coordinates of static targets into the TAMPS system aboard ship, or at MAG-11's Al Jaber base in Kuwait, and these were in turn transferred to the Hornet's mission computer via the MU or MDL. Once the target sets had been downloaded, the aircraft would allocate single aim points to each J-weapon prior to launch. Employment of the jet's radar and NITE Hawk Forward-Looking Infra-Red (FLIR) pod, as well as other external data links and/or secure radio communications from FACs/FAC(A)s, E-2s, E-3s, E-8 J-STARS, RC-135s or RQ-1 Predator UAVs, allowed the pilot to re-programme his JDAM in flight.

Aside from its stunning accuracy in OEF, the weapon also proved popular with crews because it could be released in level flight from high altitude, thus allowing aircraft to stay above SAM and AAA threats. Depending on the height and speed of the delivery platform, JDAM can be released up to 15 miles away from its target in ideal conditions.

Following several embarrassing targeting failures of LGBs in OSW in the late summer of 2002, including one which almost severed an oil pipeline, CAOC began to favour the employment of JDAM weaponry almost exclusively. This continued right up until Coalition forces pushed into Iraq on 20 March 2003 to signal the start of OIF.

VMFA-323 dropped a total of 23 1000-lb GBU-35 JDAM fitted with either standard Mk 83 or BLU-110 penetrator warheads between 19 December 2002 and 20 March 2003. During that same period the unit also expended 52 Psychological Dispersal Units, each filled with 15,000 information leaflets apiece. These instructed the Iraqis not to fire at Coalition aircraft, and explained that they were not targeting their homes, amongst other things. The leaflets also urged Iraqi commanders not to use WMD, and for frontline troops to desert, as well as illustrating the overwhelming firepower the Coalition could bring to bear.

The last weaponry dropped by VMFA-323 in OSW took the form of four JDAM delivered by a section of jets against a border patrol post at Ar Rutbah, in western Iraq. These jets were part of a larger CVW-2 strike on early warning radar and air defence command centres at H2 and H3 airfields on 19 March 2003. Although this mission, flown in conjunction with the insertion of Special Operations Forces (SOF) from nearby Jordan, was technically still a part of the CAOC's daily ATO for OSW, its key objectives (to neutralise the Scud missile threat against Israel) were part of CENTCOM's phased timetable for OIF.

PREPARATIONS ASHORE

By 19 March 2003, VMFA-323 was not the only Marine Corps Hornet unit operating with CENTCOM. In the eastern Mediterranean,

Individually loaded onto Aero-12C weapon skids, more than 30 2000-lb GBU-31(V)2/B JDAM sit in the hangar bay of CV-64 on the eve of OIF. Although VMFA-323 did not drop a single 2000-lb JDAM in OSW, it expended 41 (at $26,712 apiece) in OIF. Most of these were dropped during the 'Shock and Awe' phase of the campaign, including two (a third bomb hung) by Capt Ravey on 22 March. He had not flown with three of these weapons attached to his jet before this mission, and he told the author;

'I was part of a division that hit revetments in bad weather at night to the northeast of Baghdad. We had to fly in fingertip formation with our navigation lights on as we approached the target due to the poor weather. We were socked in at 35,000 ft, and at that height nothing was going to touch us, hence we were able to keep our lights on. The four jets in the division – two from VFA-137 and two from VMFA-323 – dropped a total of 11 2000-lb JDAM on the target. Three of these on a Hornet was about as a heavy a bomb load as the jet could manage when embarked on a carrier – it weighed 51,000 lbs when launched in this configuration. This weapon load-out was new to me, and it felt like the tailhook was caught on something, or I had left the speed brake out as I climbed away from the carrier!' (*US Navy*)

F/A-18A+-equipped VMFA-115 was serving with CVW-3, embarked in *Harry S Truman* (see Chapter 3 for details), whilst at Al Jaber, MAG-11's five Hornet units were all set to provide close air support (CAS) for I Marine Expeditionary Force (I MEF) when it pushed into Iraq.

Preparations for the large-scale deployment of Marine TACAIR to the region had begun as far back as December 2001, when the 3rd Marine Aircraft Wing (MAW) commenced Operation Planning Team meetings. The staff at MAG-11, which would be subordinate to the 3rd MAW, started deliberate planning two months later. Following the UN Security Council passing of Resolution 1441 on 8 November 2002, which gave the Iraqi government one last chance to comply with long-standing disarmament obligations by allowing unrestricted access for weapons inspectors, MAG-11 accelerated its planning process.

One of the units earmarked for deployment was Miramar-based VMFA-232, whose CO, Lt Col Mike Burt, explained to the author how the final composition of the Hornet force in-theatre was decided;

'MAG-11's headquarters staff officers started to work out how the air group was going to be composed once in Kuwait, as it was not able to deploy as a stand alone MAG due to its ongoing commitments to CVW-2 (VMFA-323) and CVW-9 (VMFA-314), as well as *WestPAC* (VMFA(AW)-242). With three Hornet units already deployed, MAG-11 had to reach out to MAG-31 at Beaufort and pull in two units (VMFA-251 and VMFA(AW)-533) to make up the numbers. The composite MAG that was sent to Al Jaber eventually consisted of the entire HQ staff and three TACAIR units (as well as MALS-11 and the KC-130-equipped VMGR-352) from MAG-11 and two from MAG-31. The group was duly designated MAG-11 as part of the 3rd MAW.'

Al Jaber was quickly identified as the best location for the TACAIR assets of MAG-11, and a Fly-In Support Package of ordnance, servicing equipment and mission planning systems was moved from Kyrgyzstan (where it had been supporting Marine Corps TACAIR assigned to OEF) to Kuwait in December 2002. By then personnel from Marine Aviation Logistics Squadron (MALS) 11 had arrived at Al Jaber from Miramar. This unit had the responsibility of ensuring that the base infrastructure was ready in time for the arrival of the first F/A-18s in January 2003.

MALS-11 oversaw the construction of extra concrete ramp space, the erection of 408 wooden 'hardbacked' tents for the 4000+ Marines that would be based at Al Jaber by the time OIF commenced and the creation of maintenance spaces for five Hornet units. A flightline intelligence centre also had to be constructed and a Tactical Aviation Fuel Dispensing System, complete with five 50,000-gallon fuel bladders, installed.

Ordnance for MAG-11 began arriving via ammunition supply ships in November 2002, and over the next two months MALS-11 built up the weapons storage facilities at Al Jaber, Ali Al Salem and Camp Fox. It took 642 truckloads to transport the ordnance from the docks to the bases. The total weight of the ordnance moved was 11,000,000 lbs, 4,000,000 lbs of which was net explosive weight. Not since the Vietnam War had so much Marine Corps aviation ordnance been located within a 30-mile radius.

In early January 2003 the first of the eleven vessels assigned to the Navy's two Maritime Prepositioning Ships (MPS) squadrons arrived in the Kuwaiti port of Ash Shuaybah. More than 250 containers filled with

4000+ line items of equipment would be offloaded from these ships in 30 days to establish the expeditionary operations capability for the fixed-wing aircraft of the 3rd MAW. This was the first MPS offload since *Desert Storm*, and the largest ever since the MPS capability was established. An additional 1150 short tons of flight equipment was flown in aboard 18 C-5s, four C-17s and two military-chartered Boeing 747F freighters.

On 21 January, the MAG-11 HQ and squadron advanced parties arrived at Al Jaber. Amongst their number was Capt Ed Bahret of VMFA(AW)-225, who recalled;

'The base was still very much a bare bones facility when we flew in. It was impressive to see just what MALS-11 and the Navy's Seabee Readiness Group could do with the site in just a matters of weeks. They poured tons of concrete in order to create a pad big enough to house all of the MAG-11 aircraft, working virtually non-stop for a full two-and-a-half months in order to achieve this prior to the war commencing.

'My squadron was the first of the MAG-11 units to fly into Al Jaber, arriving in late January. At that point there were few facilities available to us. Indeed, our maintenance shack initially consisted of a two-room tent similar in size to one that you might go camping in! Despite this, our groundcrews did an outstanding job, having jets combat loaded and ready for operations just 48 hours after reaching Al Jaber. Our maintenance people also helped oversee the arrival of the remaining MAG-11 units, as well as the two Hornet squadrons that were seconded to the group from MAG-31 for OIF.'

VMFA-232 was the next unit to arrive at Al Jaber, followed closely by VMFA(AW)-121. Like VMFA(AW)-225, both these squadrons hailed from Miramar. As the first Marine Corps outfit to convert from the A-6 Intruder to the F/A-18D in 1990, VMFA(AW)-121 had been the only two-seat Hornet unit to see combat in *Desert Storm*. Having returned to the region in 2000 for OSW, more recently it had also been the sole Marine F/A-18 squadron sent to Kyrgyzstan in support of OEF. Squadron pilot Maj Jeff Ertwine was a veteran of the Afghanistan deployment, and he explained how his unit prepared for OIF;

'We had a fair idea that we would be heading to Kuwait soon as our six-month-long OEF deployment came to an end in October 2002. A clear indication came when certain maintenance equipment and munitions that we had brought with us for OEF did not come back to Miramar when we returned home. Instead, it was shipped straight to Al Jaber.

'One of the key elements in our training immediately prior to the OIF deployment was the effort made by the squadron to get several more crews FAC(A) qualified. We knew that such personnel were going to be in great demand once the ground war started, and the unit was a little light on FAC(A)s after the Kyrgyzstan tour. You need immense situational awareness to perform this mission, as well as considerable experience in the jet, and we had guys who had plenty of both following OEF. This meant that we could train them up quickly and get them FAC(A) qualified in the three-and-a-half months that we were at home. We could not conduct this type of training whilst in Kyrgyzstan, hence the fact we had to work really hard to turn crews around at Miramar.'

On 12 February VMFA-251 became, the fifth, and last, Hornet unit to forward deploy from continental USA to Al Jaber, trailing fellow

F/A-18Cs of VMFA-232 and F/A-18Ds of VMFA(AW)-121 share ramp space at Al Jaber soon after the units' arrival in Kuwait in early February 2003. In the background can be seen some of the HASs on base that were rendered unusable after they suffered direct hits with LGBs during *Desert Storm*. This airfield was one of several occupied by the IrAF following the invasion of Kuwait by Iraqi armed forces in August 1990. The HASs, built out of reinforced concrete, have never been repaired. Maj Jeff Ertwine flew into Al Jaber with VMFA(AW)-121 in early February 2003, and he recalled;

'The unit had passed through Al Jaber in May 2002 during our flight to Kyrgyzstan, and when we returned in February 2003 we were all astounded at just how much the facility had grown in less than a year. We were the third Hornet unit to arrive at the base, and we were collected from the jets by a bus. The driver told us to throw our gear onto the vehicle and then he took us to the "tent city". The latter was huge, and he simply dropped us off and drove away! We had no idea where our tents were – it was nighttime, and there were no lights anywhere. We had all our flight gear, and we spent the next 30 minutes feeling our way around in the dark looking for our tent!

'There were rows of tents ten-long, back-to-back, with walkways criss-crossing between them. There were 400+ tents in total, with 10-12 people per tent. I was used to living in tents, having spent six months in one in Kyrgyzstan the previous year. However, that was an Air Force tent, which had air conditioning, heating and reliable electricity. At Al Jaber, we were housed in austere Marine Corps tents' (*VMFA-232*)

MAG-31 squadron VMFA(AW)-533 into Kuwait by several days. By then MAG-11 had started committing jets to the daily ATO generated by the CAOC as part of OSW. The first unit to conduct a mission into Iraq was VMFA-232 on 7 February, and squadron CO Lt Col Mike Burt detailed the types of sorties flown by his pilots prior to OIF;

'We commenced flying OSW missions on day four after the jets had arrived at Al Jaber. The squadron performed defensive counter-air (DCA) patrols, as well as providing fighter escorts for the Advanced Tactical Aerial Reconnaissance System (ATARS) F/A-18Ds that were flying missions over southern Iraq. We would send either a single jet or a two-ship section on these ATARS flights, depending on aircraft availability, the F/A-18D's mission profile and what other Coalition assets were then in-country. If there was a full DCA package on-station at the time, for example, we only needed to send a single jet in with the ATARS platform. If not, then a section of Hornets would be sortied.

'Although we flew a handful of ATARS escort missions, most of our OSW flying took the form of RO patrols. This was great training for us, as we had not done a whole lot of flying with JDAM and JSOW prior to deploying. We were occasionally called on to drop bombs for real against targets in southern Iraq, and even if we weren't, we still derived considerable training value out of each and every flight, as we always launched with simulated targets loaded into the mission computer. Such flight profiles meant that pilots got experience of running through all the switchology associated with J-weapons, short of arming the weapon up and dropping it. We repeated these missions on a daily basis until the war started. Working with the FLIR and LGBs also became a priority too.

'This focus on flying missions and employing weapons systems that we didn't use regularly when at home paid dividends for us once OIF started.

'VMFA-232 became the first unit in MAG-11 to expend ordnance in OSW when my XO and his wingman hit a cable repeater site with 1000-lb JDAM following the actioning of an RO on 16 February 2003. They had been briefed about these targets, and several others, prior to take-off, so it was a simple matter of flying to their aim points and releasing their ordnance after being given the radio call "Execute Response Option, Execute Response Option" from their AWACS controller.

'Both Hornets were part of a bigger package of jets that had flowed into the "Box" (as Coalition aircrew dubbed the No-Fly Zone), and within this formation of aircraft were designated RO bomb droppers who would be called on first should a target need to be hit.'

VMFA-232's Capt Byron Sullivan recalled that he and his fellow pilots soon got used to conducting RO strikes following this first JDAM drop;

'These types of missions quickly became old hat for us after the first couple of weeks in-theatre. Initially, when jets returned to base without their bombs everyone would run out to the flightline to quiz the pilot about what he had hit, and invariably it was a stupid repeater box alongside a highway somewhere north of Basra – the same one that we had hit two weeks earlier that they had now put back up again!'

Maj Charles Dockery of VMFA(AW)-121 also flew a number of OSW patrols from Al Jaber in the lead up to war;

'I found that the OSW missions that we were flying in 2003 were still very similar to those that I had performed three years earlier. You would put in your route to the CAOC and they would in turn tell you of potential targets that you might encounter whilst in the "Box". The missions now had a lot more meaning, however, as you knew that the ground forces were beginning to mass in Kuwait for the impending war – indeed, we flew over the ever-expanding Army and Marine camps every day as we headed into the "Box". We now spent a lot more time looking at exactly what the Iraqis had on the ground in the areas that we were patrolling. We knew that every target that we hit in southern Iraq in the final weeks of OSW would go some way to helping the troops on the ground when they pushed across the border.

'Our unit did no direct battlefield preparation strikes in the lead up to OIF though. Instead, we were hitting traditional OSW command, control and communications targets such as cable repeater stations between Basra and Baghdad. We were very frustrated at the time, as we knew something was coming, and we wanted to prep the battlefield, but I think CENTCOM stuck rigidly to its OSW target list so as to not alert the Iraqis that war was imminent.'

ATARS

As previously mentioned by Lt Col Mike Burt, some of the most important pre-war missions flown by the MAG-11 jets were the near-daily ATARS overflights over southern Iraq. Capt Ed Bahret of VMFA(AW)-225 was a subject matter expert (SME) on ATARS, and he

VMFA-232's colour jet, 'Devil 01' (F/A-18C BuNo 163481), drops away from the tanker after refuelling during an OSW DCA mission in mid March 2003. Boasting AIM-120C and AIM-9M missiles, this fighter-only configuration was abandoned within days of OIF commencing when it was realised that the IrAF was not going to contest control of Iraqi airspace. The first single-seat unit to arrive at Al Jaber, VMFA-232 initially had to manage in-theatre without most of its maintainers, as CO Lt Col Mike Burt explained;

'The rest of the unit did not arrive at Al Jaber until 9 February. For the intervening eight days, our 12 jets were maintained by six maintainers who had flown across just ahead of us as an advanced party. Fortunately, the maintainers for VMFA(AW)-225 arrived en masse in-theatre 48 hours after we showed up, so they were tasked with servicing the aircraft of all three Hornet units then at Al Jaber until additional groundcrew were flown in. The borrowed help was crucial for us, as we started flying OSW missions almost straight away.

'It was not a conscious decision on MAG-11's behalf to send our maintainers out so long after us. It was just how the personnel airlift schedule worked out, with commercial and military flights being stretched in their efforts to cope with the ramping up of activity in the Middle East. And we did not know that our personnel and equipment were going to be so badly delayed until we were actually in Al Jaber' (*USAF*) explained to the author how these sorties were run – both for the Marine Corps and the USAF – as part of the overall No-Fly Zone mission;

'We participated in OSW missions for the Air Force-driven CAOC until mid February, when the MAG-11 leadership struck a deal with CENTCOM that allowed its units to be removed from the ATO in order to conduct "free range" preparatory sorties in support of the ground war. This was crucial, as we would be working primarily with I MEF once OIF commenced. As a quid pro quo for the CAOC granting MAG-11 unrestricted access to Iraqi air space, ATARS units had to give the Air Force a dedicated reconnaissance mission when directed by the ATO – the Air Force had no manned tactical reconnaissance aircraft within its inventory that could perform in the same way as an F/A-18D ATARS.

'I flew a number of these Air Force-dedicated missions, and easily the most memorable of them took place on 27 February 2003. This operation was deemed to be so important by the CAOC that ATARS SMEs from each of the two-seat Hornet units were dialled into this classified, priority mission. An IrAF MiG-25 "Foxbat" was suspected of having landed at a military airfield in western Iraq after entering the restricted No-Fly Zone, and CENTCOM wanted proof. This mission had been urgently requested by the CAOC so as to provide Air Force strike aircraft with quick targeting imagery of the MiG-25 so that they could in turn rapidly destroy it, thus demonstrating to the Iraqis that CENTCOM had the ability to conduct time-sensitive targeting (TST).

'I was given a special waiver to break my crew duty day of 12 hours to help plan and lead this hop. At the time of our planned return, my duty day would be over 21 hours. The flight was to take off at 0130 hrs local and take about 3.5 hours to complete. Thanks to a contractor accidentally severing a power line to our planning cell, all mission-planning computers were down. Planning for the sortie was therefore conducted on a map with a string and an aeronautical slide rule on a wristwatch.

'We had to plan to get three F/A-18D Hornets to western Iraq from Kuwait with no air or SEAD (Suppression of Enemy Air Defences) support. Indeed, we were expected to self-escort and provide intra-flight SEAD, as well as conducting the all-important reconnaissance aspect of the mission. To make matters worse, less than an hour before take-off, the Air Force informed us that they couldn't spare the tankers to get us to the target area and back. In light of this news, we were going to scrap the flight, but the Air Force made it a "priority mission".

'We hastily reconfigured the jets with three external fuel tanks and two AIM-9Ms for self-defence, and removed the HARM, and their pylons, so as to reduce the wing drag, and therefore save fuel. By our calculations we would all flame out before reaching base if we flew at tactical air speeds.

'To solve this problem, we flew fuel conservation profiles similar to an airliner. For recap, so far we were alone, low on fuel, tired, going far, far from base, flying profiles that asked for us to be shot at and only had two AIM-9Ms apiece for self-defence – don't forget that this mission was also being performed at the death hour of the morning. Damn, if nothing else I just wanted to see how this "circus act" ended up!

'Ingress was tense, but uneventful. The target area was extremely quiet – almost too quiet for a suspected landing site of a valuable MiG-25 fighter. We were expecting some form of greeting, but nothing. The stillness of the morning put the question in our minds, "is it really down there, or is this just a wild goose chase?" Egress was tenser still, since we hawked the fuel gauge every other second. Baghdad could be seen all lit up on the distant horizon to our north.

'The radio was quiet, for nobody else was up at the time (indeed, it was meant to be an OSW no-fly day for us), until the tracking radar of an SA-6 "Gainful" SAM gave my ship a critical lock indication, meaning that the battery had locked onto my jet and was about to fire, if they had not already done so. A rapid crew coordination meeting was scheduled and conducted, lasting about three seconds from start to finish, to put out chaff and flares, but not to manoeuvre unless we saw a missile guiding on us. We had to save fuel, as we either had fuel to cruise home or to threat react, but not both. When exiting the "Box", we conducted a mission handover with two RAF Tornado GR 4As heading for the same target. We made it home with less than 1100 lbs of our 16,700 lbs of fuel.

'The net result of this mission was that the tapes to record the images failed – an all too regular occurrence with ATARS in OSW/OIF – and we got nothing. That was not the end of the story, however, for I had told the aircrew to record all displays and provide a running mission commentary to the recorders to help the maintenance Marines troubleshoot the recce systems. Fortunately, the cockpit tapes recorded the SAR (Synthetic Aperture Radar) mapping pages of the images that we tried to take.

'Once back at Al Jaber, I helped the Intel Marines of MAG-11 produce a mosaic from video captures of the displays to confirm that the airfield that the MiG-25 was suspected to have landed at was covered with barricades, fences and corner reflectors, rendering the runways unusable. End state – the MiG was never found. The fog of war, I guess. For the aircrews' efforts we got sleeping pills from the flight surgeon, since we had been up for over 30 hours. Good night!

'We were quite critical of the Air Force in our post-mission debrief because they had asked us to perform this mission at short notice, but had not supplied us with any support in respect to tankers, SEAD or CAPs.

'Although these Air Force-driven sorties appeared regularly on the ATO, the vast majority of our ATARS flights in OSW were performed for I MEF, which needed as much intelligence as possible on Iraqi troop emplacements and defensive positions along the Kuwaiti border. The imagery we gleaned was fed directly to the troops preparing for OIF.

'ATARS has the ability to capture imagery via electro-optical (EO) and infrared (IR) sensors, as well as SAR. This equipment allowed I MEF intelligence folks to build up a picture of enemy territory, revealing minefields, camouflaged artillery or tanks hidden in camouflaged hides. Regular ATARS missions revealed patterns of movement along the Iraqi-Kuwaiti border, the recce equipment being so sensitive that it could detect disturbed dirt left behind by either a wheeled or tracked vehicle.

'The ATARS mission is not a sexy one, being far removed from the Hollywood idea of the fast jet pilot shooting down the enemy, or the precision bomber with his "greatest hits" videos of Baghdad. The ATARS mission is, however, going to give the battlefield commander intelligence about his enemy that will hopefully save Marines' lives in the long run.

'Although ATARS is not the most modern or advanced system being fielded by the US military today, its shortcomings were more than compensated for in OIF by the rapid-response tactical reconnaissance capabilities of our aircraft. We could move into an area faster than a Predator, and we were also safer in a combat zone than a UAV, which could be shot down quite easily by barrage fire once detected.

'Being a manned reconnaissance asset, we also had the ability to make an on-scene assessment of what it was the jet was seeing through its sensors. The UAV could not do this, as the images of the target that it sends back to its operator give the latter little more than a soda straw view of the area being over-flown. Being FAC(A) qualified, I could use all the sensors in the jet to gain crucial situational awareness for the commander on the ground in advance of returning to base with the target imagery.

'The primary recording device in the ATARS is the 19 mm tape, which collects images digitally and allows them to be expeditiously played back once the jet has returned to base. The WSO simply presses record on his ATARS control panel as the jet passes over the target coordinates, which have been derived via GPS in order to ensure total mission accuracy. The equipment requires time to record the image onto the tape, however, and it also takes time to exploit it once on the ground. We have two tapes that are installed in the jet prior to take-off, and these record imagery from all three recce sensors – IR, EO and SAR.

'The three imagery sensors in the jet are built to fulfil different target requirements. If I am asked to go and find tanks dispersed in a defensive pattern I won't choose to use EO, as that only works during daylight. If they are under camouflage netting in the desert, then I won't be able to see them in daylight. Therefore, IR would be the best sensor to use, as it will detect a heat source from the tanks, day or night – as long as you avoid flying the mission during the thermal crossover period at dawn or dusk.

'Normally, we would only want to make a single reconnaissance run over the target unless we felt that we had not captured the desired imagery. I can review the tape in the cockpit following the target pass, allowing me to quickly determine whether we have to make a second run. If I find something significant on the tape, and require better resolution to determine exactly what it is I am looking at, then we will make a second pass. The pilot will usually lower his height, increase his speed and approach the target from a different direction when conducting the

Storeless VMFA(AW)-533 F/A-18D BuNo 164957 heads back to Al Jaber in early March 2003 after expending its single JDAM during an RO strike in the 'Box'. Although usually uneventful, the near-daily OSW missions flown by the MAG-11 Hornet squadrons into the 'Box' were crucial to the units' pre-OIF preparations, as Capt Ed Bahret of VMFA(AW)-225 recalled;

'An important aspect of this early deployment phase was getting all the new aircrew in the unit used to hearing all the radio communication that was synonymous with operating in-theatre. Getting these guys past the general confusion and "fog of war" that the secure radio "comms" could create in OSW was critical for the subsequent mission effectiveness of the squadron in the early stages of OIF. We therefore made a conscious effort to ensure that the new guys got into the "Box" during OSW in order to get them over this "comms" hump' (Maj Doug Glover)

F/A-18D BuNo 165531 was one of three ATARS jets assigned to VMFA(AW)-225. These aircraft were kept very busy during OSW and OIF, hence the weathered appearance of this jet. The success rate achieved by the ATARS crews in the missions flown from Al Jaber has been hotly debated since OIF, although Capt Doug Glover of VMFA(AW)-533 was effusive about the system post-war;

'ATARS was a great asset to the Marine Corps during OSW/OIF. Even with the tape reliability issues that we had (failure rates ran at 50 per cent), the amount of usable imagery generated by ATARS flights, coupled with the number of targets discovered, made the system worth the inevitable pain of a tape that failed to record, or which corrupted the data from one camera. The problem that was most difficult to solve was the dissemination of the imagery in a timely manner. We had a high-speed datalink between I MEF and the 3rd MAW at Al Jaber, but the link below I MEF level was of a much more low-tech variety. Indeed, imagery was often simply printed out and handed to the Marines in hard-copy form, thereby negating the advantages of a scrollable, digital image file.'

VMFA(AW)-121's Capt Charles Dockery was less enthusiastic;

'Mission tasking from the CAOC wasn't very good, as on the few ATARS missions that I flew I was never given specific information about what it was I needed to get imagery of. The running of the ATARS mission as a whole was never set in stone, so we had no real idea who we were supposed to talk to prior to the mission, during the actual sortie and in the all important post-mission imagery exploitation phase' (*Capt Ed Bahret*)

second pass in an effort to throw off the aim of any potential defenders who may want to protect the target from detection.

'Typically, our pass heights over the target were dictated by the weather in the immediate area. We also had to avoid dropping down into the various weapon engagement zones which proliferated across southern Iraq. Although these zones were off limits for TACAIR assets that were conducting OSW patrols, we were given permission to descend into them for a short period of time in order to complete our reconnaissance passes.

'Although there were reports of us being shot at during these missions by crews from nearby F-15Es or controllers of Predator UAVs (both platforms had better FLIR pods than us), I rarely saw any AAA – 60 mm rounds I couldn't see with the naked eye, but 100 mm shells were visible. There were the occasional "puffies" from rounds exploding nearby, but it was hardly like World War 2! Those platforms that could see the AAA were usually identifying its presence through their FLIR pods, which spotted muzzle flashes from known artillery positions near the target area.

'We initially ranged all over southern Iraq conducting reconnaissance flights, being given free rein to fly virtually anywhere within the OSW No-Fly Zone. However, once we rolled into performing reconnaissance missions directly for I MEF, we were tasked with flying beyond the 33rd parallel as the ground forces needed intelligence on what lay ahead of them deeper into Iraq. The plan for the ground war in OIF called for rapid advancement at the start of the campaign, hence the need for ATARS imagery of enemy territory nearer to Baghdad.

'The pressing urgency for reconnaissance imagery also meant that ATARS jets were the only Coalition aircraft given clearance by the CAOC to fly directly over Basra during OSW. Such a mission was considered to be rather risky, and no other fast jets were permitted to do this until OIF commenced. The information gleaned from these Basra overflights was passed directly on to the Royal Marines, who needed detailed imagery of the southern city, as well as the nearby Al Faw peninsula, as it was their responsibility to seize this area once the war started. Helicopters from the 3rd MAW would help airlift the Royal Marines into key locations around the city, and we provided the intelligence on the various landing sites that they required.

'When given an ATARS mission during OSW, we would usually get tasking via the ATO 24 hours prior to flying the sortie. Typically, staff intelligence officers from either the CAOC or I MEF would tell us what they were looking for. They already had good intelligence on where the major Iraqi Army divisions were situated, but they needed up-to-date imagery of any new defensive positions in buildings or along fortified perimeters, as well as changes in the artillery formations. The intelligence officers were also looking for signs that the Iraqis were preparing to send forces south from Baghdad to reinforce those troops already in the region. We would be given a general idea of what to look for, and then once over Iraq we would methodically overfly the area seeking out visible changes.

'The aircrew was given free rein to make up their flight plan so as to get the required imagery, with intelligence officers indicating what they would like us to specifically look at. For a typical Basra mission, for example, they might ask us to look at a certain area within the nearby port facility, or where the Tigris and Euphrates rivers meet. They didn't care how we got to the target area, but they were very specific about what they wanted us to photograph. We therefore planned our route to and from the target area, checking with the CAOC as to exactly where we were allowed to fly in respect to the various weapons engagement zones that surrounded the objective.

'Due to the way the ATARS works, and the way reconnaissance missions are flown in general, we would be faced with lots of straight and level flight time in enemy territory. Reconnaissance jets have to follow a very predictable flight path in order to get the imagery that is required. We would almost always sortie into Iraqi airspace with a fighter escort – usually a second F/A-18D from the squadron armed with AIM-9Ms and AMRAAM. If the target was deemed to be high priority, then two ATARS jets were despatched, both of which had a dedicated fighter escort provided by one of the single-seat Hornet units at Al Jaber.

'In order to speed up the flow of information, we would immediately take our image tapes to squadron-provided exploitation ground stations, rather than suffering delays by having the analysis done at higher command level. Our ATARS specialists would quickly ascertain whether the mission was a success or not. Often, they would see a trend in movements or defensive construction that meant that we would have to head back to the target area for a follow-up photo-run the very next day.

'In OSW, a lot of the senior commanders in CENTCOM for whom we were trying to get this imagery had no real idea of what we could produce with ATARS. They had never seen ATARS imagery before, and had therefore not trained to incorporate the system into their battle planning. When they were told that there were ATARS jets now in-theatre, the senior officers really had little idea of how best to exploit this asset. However, once CENTCOM's Coalition Forces Air Component Commander (CFACC) saw the fully exploited images – complete with target coordinates – produced by the intelligence team at Al Jaber, his staff quickly realised that ATARS could provide them with something that they could use in the their OIF battle planning.

'A lack of corporate knowledge on the system meant that we took a while to ramp up the ATARS flights during OSW. We were also badly affected by the failure of our in-flight datalink which could have provided imagery in near-real time to I MEF command centres in the field – a cure for these software problems was finally found just days after OIF ended.

'MAG-11 initially struggled with ATARS, as the Marine Corps had never really figured out the best way to employ it. Indeed, the system had only been in frontline service for about 18 months by the time OIF rolled around. The system is old, having been developed in 1981, and it relies on temperamental 19 mm tapes similar in design to videocassettes for recording imagery – tape failure rates approached 50 per cent in OIF.

'Although it proved a slow process to get the ATARS mission up and running, once we started using the equipment on a daily basis, the reliability of the system drastically improved. Indeed, I MEF ultimately gleaned a lot of intelligence from our ATARS material during OSW.'

WAR PLANNING

Imagery that Capt Bahret and his fellow SMEs were collecting in their ATARS jets was indeed being put to good use by staff officers in I MEF HQ, who were working out the final details of their portion of OIF.

Pentagon war planners had presented the tactical model OPLAN 1003V to the US government as being the best way to ensure that OIF was a swift campaign with minimal collateral damage to civilians and the country's infrastructure. The opening phase of the campaign would see fixed targets across Iraq overwhelmed by air strikes in the 'Shock and Awe' phase of the war. Several days later, mechanised troops from the US Army's V Corps and the Marine Corps' I MEF would push into Iraq from Kuwait, hell-bent on reaching Baghdad as quickly as possible.

The Marine Air-Ground Task Force (MAGTF), consisting of I MEF, the 1st MARDIV and the 3rd MAW, would be responsible for seizing the eastern half of Iraq. After being briefed on the Marine Air proposal for supporting the ground war in the east, CENTCOM's CFACC, USAF Lt Gen T Michael Mosely, gave the plan his full backing. This meant that the 3rd MAW would be allowed to support the MAGTF first, rather than having to allocate large numbers of sorties to the joint air campaign, as had been the case in *Desert Storm*.

Conversely, the adoption of this plan placed a heavy burden on MAG-11's 60 Hornets at Al Jaber, as they would be almost exclusively responsible for providing CAS support to the ground component of the MAGTF. To ensure that the aircrew manning these jets were fully aware of what was required of them, joint CAS procedures and training with all MAG units and Division FACs and Air Officers was carried out at the Udairi range in the weeks leading up to OIF. One of those to benefit from the exercises was F/A-18 pilot Capt Brian Foster, who was serving as a FAC with Bravo Company, 2nd Battalion, 5th Marine Regiment;

'For most Marine TACAIR pilots, you have one tour in the frontline in jets which is then followed by a disassociated tour away from flying. Being a FAC is one of the things that you can do during your time out of the cockpit.

'I buddied up with the same tank crew for the duration of the campaign, with the commander of my M1A1 Abrams also being the XO of the company – he was a 1st lieutenant. I was attached to the company two weeks prior to the invasion of Iraq, conducting training with the crew in the lead up to war on the Udairi range. These exercises gave me the opportunity to practice my controlling techniques with MAG-11 assets sortied from Al Jaber. We had put out a blanket call for air support whilst on the range, and although I primarily controlled Marine Corps jets, Navy Hornets and Tomcats also made an appearance.'

Having Marine Corps pilots on the ground in the frontline controlling TACAIR assets for I MEF's five Regimental Combat Teams (RCT) would prove hugely important once OIF started, as VMFA(AW)-121's Capt Charles Dockery explained to the author;

'All the FACs that I would subsequently work with in Iraq had been previous squadron or schoolmates, or had a connection with someone in my unit. Aside from knowing these guys, we also conducted face-to-face planning meetings with the division fire support coordinator and air officer prior to OIF commencing. By conducting these division "huddles" pre-war, we then knew what the ground troops would be doing once they entered Iraq, and they knew full well what we could do for them to help speed their progress north.

'The information I gleaned from these meetings also meant that I could brief my squadron on the scheme of manoeuvre from division down to infantry company level. I don't think that our Air Force compatriots got into the ground war in this kind of detail, choosing not to read the daily ground op orders – the latter gave you an indication of what the ground commander's intent was for that day, and what events may shift that effort. The Air Force lacked a personal connection with its FACs on the ground, as they generally operated with enlisted guys who had no experience as aircrew.'

The multiple MAGTF training/coordination meetings that Capt Dockery mentioned were routinely conducted to ensure that aircrew were absolutely clear about what I MEF commander, Lt Gen James T Conway, intended to do once he entered Iraq, and the levels of support that he was expecting from the 3rd MAW for his overall scheme of manoeuvre.

In order to ensure that this support was available to the right units precisely when it was needed, MAG-11 assigned individual Hornet squadrons to each of the five RCTs as point of contact and planning liaison for the ground scheme of manoeuvre and aviation employment during the opening days of the impending war.

Having had the best part of two months to bed its units into Al Jaber and get its aircrew familiar with how the CAOC ran things in-theatre, MAG-11 was now ready for 'G-Day' – the commencement of the ground phase of OIF. As previously mentioned, this was supposed to follow at least 72 hours after the first 'Shock and Awe' 'A-Day' strikes, but last-minute changes to the plan by CENTCOM's commander, Gen Tommy Franks, actually meant that the ground war was to start 15 hours *before* the first air strikes.

Those senior enough in the 3rd MAW were told that I MEF would breach the defensive berm that separated southern Iraq from Kuwait at 0600 hrs on 21 March. However, the plan hastily changed once again on the 19th after CENTCOM saw satellite imagery of six burning oil wells in the strategically important Rumaylah oilfields, situated to the west of Basra.

Late that same day, following the issuing of the execute order for OIF by President George W Bush, MAG-11 Hornets were sent to knock out various targets in southern Iraq on the very last OSW missions ever flown. Less than 24 hours later those same jets were striking enemy forces in the same areas, but now they were participating in OIF.

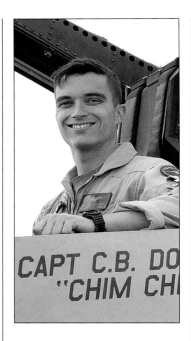

VMFA(AW)-121's WSO training officer in OSW/OIF, Capt Charles Dockery was also one of the unit's FAC(A)-qualified aircrew. The latter were literally worth their weight in gold in OIF, FAC(A) crews controlling the airspace overhead the myriad kill boxes which proliferated across Iraq. VMFA(AW)-121 boasted seven FAC(A)-qualified pilot/WSO crews in OIF, and these were regularly augmented by two more crews drawn from the ranks of the MAG-11 staff. A veteran of VMFA(AW)-121's OSW deployment in 2000, the unit's six-month spell in Kyrgyzstan two years later and, of course, OIF, Capt Dockery's impact on the squadron's warfighting capabilities earned him the Marine Corps Aviation Association's Naval Flight Officer of the Year award in 2004 (*VMFA(AW)-121*)

MAG-11 IN OIF

'Marines and sailors of this great air wing, today we were attacked by hostile Iraqi forces at several locations. This afternoon and tonight both fixed wing and rotary wing strike elements from our air groups will attack Iraq positions across the border, and thus begin the campaign to remove Saddam Hussein and his regime from power and return Iraq to its people.

'The courage and skills of this air wing will be tested. We will not be found wanting! You are called upon to join the ranks of those brave Marines who have gone before you. You have trained hard, you have sacrificed, you are ready. As you take this fight to the enemy and lead our great nation into combat, I offer you these thoughts;

'I am honoured to be your commander and serve in your presence.

'What we are embarking on is an honourable cause, and we will prove that to the world.

'You are much more ready and prepared than you think you are.

'Leadership and discipline will overcome the fearful and the unknown – it always has.

'There is a fear that is worse than death – that's the fear of letting down your fellow Marines. You won't.

'We will win this war and the respect of the Iraqi people, and we will do it honourably. God bless each of you, our country, and God bless the United States Marine Corps!'

This brief message by Maj Gen James F Amos, Commanding General of the 3rd MAW, was read out to all hands at Al Jaber on the evening of 20 March 2003. From now on MAG-11 was embroiled in OIF.

Earlier that same day, the Bush administration had pre-empted the official start of OIF by authorising a daring pre-dawn precision strike on Baghdad. This raid by two F-117s on three homes (also variously reported as a Republican Guard bunker and the Dora Farms compound) owned by members of the Iraqi leadership in a suburb of Baghdad had been rapidly generated following a tip-off that Saddam and four of his top commanders had been seen entering the buildings. Although the targets were destroyed by four EGBU-27 'Have Void' 2000-lb LGBs, the intelligence proved to be wrong and Saddam remained very much alive.

Minutes after the F-117s had dropped their ordnance, 40 Tomahawk Land Attack Missiles launched from US Navy warships in the NAG hit other downtown Baghdad targets, including an intelligence service HQ and a Republican Guard installation.

Prior to the decapitation strikes and the missile attacks on Kuwait, Gen Franks and his senior staff at CENTCOM had decided that 'G-Day' had to be brought forward by eight hours so as to secure the Rumaylah oilfields prior to them being torched by Iraqi troops. One of the key targets that needed to be destroyed prior to the invasion commencing was a key Iraqi observation post on Safwan Hill, which directly overlooked the assembly points for the Coalition forces in Kuwait, as well as their

Majs Jeff Ertwine (left) and Mike Waterman regularly flew together as a FAC(A)-qualified team with VMFA(AW)-121 during OIF. There were only around 20 FAC(A) crews at Al Jaber, and they were in constant demand throughout the campaign. The importance of their mission was quickly realised by their non-qualified squadronmates, as Maj Ertwine recalled;

'The biggest compliment that we got as FAC(A)s came from our executive officer. During the few months between returning from OEF and then deploying to OIF, he had a chance to either become a FAC(A) or renew his qualifications as an air combat tactics instructor. He chose the latter, so we worked him up with a series of air-to-air sorties and he got his re-certification done without any great dramas.

'About two-thirds of the way through the war he took some of us FAC(A) crews aside and told us "I wish I had gotten my FAC(A) quals instead. You guys have the backdoor pass to the war, doing all the work. And here we are flying the ATARS platform or performing the CAS mission. We're not getting the tanker support, and we are being told to check in with you guys in order to get our tasking!" His words carried even more weight because he was a single-seat Hornet guy who had come over into the two-seat community when he joined VMFA(A)-121' (*Maj Jeff Ertwine*)

breaching points for the defensive berms that separated the two countries. The earthen barrier consisted of two berms that ran the length of the Iraq-Kuwait border, with a no-man's-land of mines between them that was about a mile wide. Entry points through the berms were to be made by Marine Corps engineers, prior to I MEF pushing through.

Any activity within the berms would be visible from only one point – Safwan Hill, just south of the Rumaylah oilfields. Studded with powerful optics and antennas for looking and listening into Kuwait, it was to be MAG-11's first target in OIF, and the task of ensuring the destruction of the Iraqi positions on Safwan Hill was passed to VMFA(AW)-121, VMFA(AW)-533 and VMFA-251.

Although mission planning for this strike had been completed days earlier, no one at Al Jaber had been informed that zero hour for 'G-Day' had been brought forward. The experiences of VMFA(AW)-121's Maj Jeff Ertwine were typical for MAG-11 on the afternoon of 20 March;

'I was one of the duty pilots standing the Alert 30 for the strike on Safwan Hill when the Iraqis started shooting missiles into Kuwait. It was at this point that I realised OIF was virtually upon us. We went to the bunkers at Al Jaber three times during the afternoon of 20 March. It was utter chaos, despite the drills, as we struggled with our chem suits, and the empty bags that littered the shelter after we had donned our gear. It almost seemed like the Iraqis drove us into action with these attacks, as I thought that the push on Safwan Hill was still a day or two away.

'The guys that replaced us on the Alert had only literally walked into the crew duty tent when they were called to man up their jets and head for Safwan Hill. I was not upset that I had missed the call by just a matter of minutes, as I had been manning the Alert for eight hours, jumping out of our full flight gear and into a chem suit during this time. I was bushed, and happy to get my head down for some rest. I knew that the war was now about to kick off, and there would be plenty of combat to go around.

'When I came into work later that day, I expected to have my briefing and then head straight out on a mission. Instead, I found that the squadron's mission schedule was in utter chaos! Instead of flying, I had to sit down and rework the entire flow of sorties heading into Iraq over the next 24 hours. I handed my scheduled flight over to another pilot, as I was the only one in the ops tent who knew what was going on in respect to the sorties we were supposed to generate and the targets we had been assigned to hit via the ATO. The unit had been launching crews since the missile attacks with little more information than a call-sign to check in with once over Iraq! Chaos reigned for the first 12 hours of the war.

'Word that the war was going to start on 20 March 2003 did not reach us, or any of the other units in MAG-11 for that matter. Although we had been conducting some training flights with the ground forces, we had not been briefed on any set strikes. Hence the confusion that gripped us in the

Some 500 Mk 77 fire bomb (napalm) canisters were dropped by AV-8Bs in *Desert Storm*, but only 24 were expended in OIF – all by VMFA(AW)-225. Capt Ed Bahret told the author;

'These spectacular weapons were used purely in a psychological capacity to demoralise the enemy. There was never any intent from MAG-11's point of view to go out and actually strike a target. We flew two missions with the firebombs, and they had approval from the senior planners in the CAOC. The reasoning behind the mission was to put the fear of God into the enemy by dropping fire bombs in a nearby field so that they could see the weapons' devastating effects.

'Unfortunately, the delivery height restrictions in place over the battlefield, brought about by our keenness to stay above the MEZ, meant that the fire bombs were dropped from 10,000 ft. The best way to ensure target accuracy with this weapon, which has terrible ballistic characteristics in flight, is to drop it from 200 ft at the "speed of heat" and let it scatter and spread. On the first mission, the fire bombs produced little more than six small puddles of fuel gelatine burning in a field due to their release height!

'Following this embarrassment, the CAOC allowed us to perform a second fire bomb mission that saw the weapons dropped at below 500 ft into a field near Tallil air base, west of An Nasiriyah. Six jets were sortied, each of which was armed with three canisters. Flying in a near line abreast formation, the F/A-18Ds simply ran across a wide-open field and simultaneously dropped their weapons' (*Capt Ed Bahret*)

first hours after the missiles hit. There were a lot of people jumping through their rear ends at Al Jaber trying to figure out what was going on.'

In spite of this confusion, VMFA(AW)-121 at least knew that Safwan Hill had to be hit, and the man tasked with leading the mission was squadron CO, Lt Col Matt Shihadeh;

'Maj "Sweet P" Petersen and I had been planning the Safwan strike for more than a week. The idea was to hit the buildings on Safwan Hill and to the east of the hill at the same time that Marine Corps Cobras were hitting the border posts. A few minutes later, 1 Marine Recon would be helicopter-inserted on top of the hill to kill anyone remaining (and a section of our aircraft would remain on-station with 20 mm cannon for suppression). Once the observation posts were taken down, the grunts could cross the border without the enemy being able to hit them with effective (i.e., observed) artillery fire.

'Crews had been standing Alert for the Safwan mission for several days, and in the early evening of the 20th, this duty was shared by two pilots and WSOs from my squadron and two crews from VMFA(AW)-533. The phone rang in the Alert tent at 1730 hrs, and I was told by the MAG-11 operations officer that we were to launch immediately for an 1830 time on target (TOT). I wasn't sure that there was enough time to make that TOT, but I told him that we were walking to the jets.

'We had some problems getting everybody out of the line, with one of my crews having GPS and MU issues that almost caused us to leave them behind. Indeed, we taxied without them, but they soon followed us as their jet "got well" while taxiing.

'"Sweet P" and I then had a JDAM "Fail" indication on our Station 8 weapon, so we did some fast typing in the hold-short to assign the weapon on Station 3 to that DMPI (Designated Mean Point of Impact). We were all carrying four bombs, but only planned on each dropping three.

Despite our best efforts, we did not actually take-off until 1830 hrs, and once airborne there were all sorts of "comms" problems. We got tired of trying to get a hold of the command and control agencies and just switched up the mission frequency to talk to the airborne mission commander (a lieutenant-colonel in a Huey). It took four different frequencies, but we were finally able to reach him. He asked what our TOT would be and we told him 1845 hrs. From the sounds of their frantic "comm", the helicopters were having a lot of trouble keeping sight

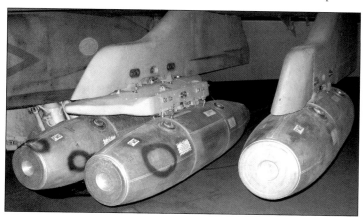

of each other (limited visibility due to blowing dust).

'We pickled 14 (vice the planned 15) 2000-lb GBU-31s JDAM at 1844 hrs. One of the VMFA(AW)-533 aircraft had a problem with its JDAM and was only able to drop two. On the FLIR, we were able to see our first two bombs hit and blow up their DMPIs (HQ building to the east of the hill), but our third bomb was a dud (although it went right through the building that it was supposed to hit). Using the

FLIR's Wide Field-Of-View, we were able to see the other explosions on the east DMPIs, and on top of the hill.

'Since we were left with an asymmetric load (bomb on the outboard station), we elected to leave Dash-2 and -3 in the target area for suppression (instead of us and Dash-2). They didn't end up having to suppress anything, but they did observe the Cobras destroying a vehicle that was trying to escape from the top of the hill and head north.

'The helicopters ended up cancelling their insert due to the crappy weather. They tried again early the next morning, but again the weather was a no-go. The grunts got across the border that morning (21st) and found Safwan Hill deserted.'

Firebomb-toting F/A-18Cs from VMFA-251 were supposed to follow up the F/A-18D strikes in order to finish off the entrenched troops dug in around the remaining border posts just beyond the breaching points for the 1st MARDIV. However, a combination of poor weather and confused TACAIR control in the opening hours of the campaign resulted in the unit never making it to Safwan Hill. Instead, a late call went out to VMFA-232, and one of the pilots scrambled was Capt Byron Sullivan;

'Capt "Val" Vranish and I were manning an Alert at Al Jaber, and we had little inkling beforehand that we would be flying that night. Indeed, we weren't even strapped into our jets when I made the call to the TACC (Tactical Air Command Center, which was the senior Marine Corps agency in control of MAG-11 jets) to let them know that the Alert was set. The voice on the other end of the telephone came straight back with coordinates for a target that the CAOC needed hit within 25 minutes!

'We ran to our jets, took off and literally as soon as we had our "wheels in the well" we started talking to the first of four controlling agencies. Ten minutes later we were finally being passed onto our FAC, who just happened to be an ex-VMFA-232 Hornet pilot. He was situated about a mile-and-a-half to the west of the target. We climbed up to 17,000 ft at around 350 knots. The weather was terrible, but he had good coordinates that allowed us to perform a section roll into the clouds as soon as we crossed the border into Iraq. We relied exclusively on the FAC's coordinates, as we could not see the target because of the weather. We simultaneously dropped two sticks of three Mk 83 dumb bombs with great accuracy into entrenched troops and a bunker on Safwan Hill.

'Friendly troops had started taking artillery fire directed by spotters on Safwan Hill just prior to pushing across the border, and when a requested air strike by VMFA-251 had not shown up, they had a Time-on-Target that needed to be met and we got the call. The mission duration was so short – total flight time 27 minutes – that we had to dump gas before we could land!'

Aside from the dedicated Safwan Hill strikers, other Hornets were

A VMFA(AW)-533 jet breaks away from Capt Doug Glover's Hornet during a section patrol of Iraq in late March 2003. This aircraft is manned by a non-FAC(A)-qualified crew, as it lacks the tell-tale tubes for the 'Willie-Pete' five-inch rockets which were used to mark targets in kill boxes throughout OIF. LMAVs were also favoured by FAC(A) crews. This jet is armed with a GBU-16B/B LGB and a GBU-32/B JDAM – both 1000-lb weapons – on its port wing pylons, and a solitary 500 Mk 82 'dumb' bomb on the starboard wing outer pylon. Boasting a single AIM-120C and AIM-9M for self-defence, the aircraft is devoid of a NITE Hawk targeting pod (*Maj Doug Glover*)

also scrambled from Al Jaber and sent into action over Iraq. VMFA(AW)-225's Capt Ed Bahret was in the back of one of the first F/A-18Ds launched by his unit;

'Despite our base having been under attack by missiles for much of the afternoon of the 20th, we were all sat in one of the bunkers on base, with my section still manning the Alert 30 jets in support of OSW – we had still to be informed that OIF had started. We did know, however, that there were Special Operations Forces (SOF) teams in Iraq, and that was why we were manning the Alert in case they need us for CAS.

'We duly received a call to report to the group operations centre, where we were told that missiles had fallen near the Sharq Mall in Kuwait City. The MAG-11 operations officer told us, "Gentleman, we're stepping. Get in your jets and take off. Do not talk to this controlling agency but go straight to this agency and they will give you your tasking. Good hunting Marines. *Sempi Fi*!" He shook our hands and we ran for our jets.

'When the first wave of missiles had hit Kuwait, we had launched our first section of jets, one of which was flown by the CO. Twenty minutes later we were scrambled, and told to check in with a ground controller who was in contact with a British SAS operative who had followed the mobile launcher that had apparently fired the first missile at Kuwait City. My CO's section had actually been the first on scene over Basra in response to the call for TACAIR to hit the launcher, but they had experienced NITE Hawk FLIR pod failure, so they had cleared the airspace over the city and left the target wide open for us.

'As with our ultimately fruitless Air Force ATARS mission on 27 February, CENTCOM was keen to send a message to the Iraqi leadership that we could find TSTs such as missile launchers very fast and take them out, unlike in *Desert Storm*. Our controller was asking us to find – now get this – a camouflaged truck under camouflage netting that was strung across a single lane road between two suspected houses in the middle of the city! It was a no-moon night, with complete undercast at 11,000 ft, and everybody with AAA and a slingshot was trying for us.

Having donned their chemical warfare suits and gas masks, MAG-11 personnel take refuge in one of the numerous shelters built at Al Jaber. This photograph was taken by VMFA(AW)-225's Capt Ed Bahret during the Iraqi missile attacks on Kuwait during the afternoon of 20 March 2003. His section manned the squadron's Alert 30 jets throughout these strikes, and he was eventually scrambled at dusk and sent to Basra to knock out one of the mobile missile launchers responsible for the attacks (*Capt Ed Bahret*)

VMFA(AW)-225's BuNo 164677 leads a second 'Vikings' F/A-18D on a dusk sortie into Iraq during the opening phase of OIF. The unit was heavily involved in providing CAS support for I MEF and Royal Marine forces tasked with seizing Umm Qasar airfield, Safwan Hill, Safwan airfield, the all-important Rumaylah oilfields and the Al Faw peninsula in the opening 48 hours of the war (*Capt Ed Bahret*)

'Our no-lower-than limit altitude was 15,000 ft due to our restrictions of flight operations at the time. Upon our first pass, I informed the controller that we couldn't see the target due to the weather. He then asked us to stand by. Right, I'll just circle a target and enjoy those AAA sparkles passing my jet till you get back to me. We told him we were departing the area till he called back. He said we were cleared, by higher authority, to disregard the altitude restriction and "find the launcher".

'We proceeded below the weather rather reluctantly, since we were highlighted by the lights of the city against the undercast, and started to search the given Latitude-Longitude coordinates. After several passes, we could not find the target, and questioned if it was there. We were informed that the SAS agent was now looking at the target. Unfortunately, he did not have a laser designator to paint it. He asked us to drop on the coordinate, to which we responded with a resounding "Hell No!" The 1st MARDIV's Judge Advocate General (JAG) lawyer, and the world's press, would have had us served up on a silver platter if we dropped a 1000-lb LGB without laser guidance into a residential area with only the assumption that the target was where the spotter said it was.

'As we later found out, the SAS operative was not giving us a precise coordinate. Rather, he only had a map, and was using the "TLAR" ("That Looks About Right") method of targeting.

'We ended up leaving the area, and the target was never serviced. I know that the SAS operative was more than a little frustrated, as he had eyes on the launcher. He had no laser designator, so we would have been forced to self-designate. In order to do this with any accuracy we had to be able to see the target with our sensor, which we could not – even after six passes over Basra. With each pass we got lower and lower, and by the final run over the coordinates we were below 10,000 ft. This was 5000 ft under the height restriction that was then in place for TACAIR assets over Iraq.

'Having failed to find the launcher, we left Basra and headed for an artillery position near the refinery in the Rumaylah oilfields – our CO had also headed for this target following his pod failure. The battery was too close to the refinery for us to drop a bomb on it, however, so we ended up returning to base with all three of our Mk 82 LGBs still under the wings.

'The RoE in place at the start of the war was simply too restrictive for us to go out and hit these targets on the opening night of OIF. Should there be any doubt about the identity of the target, then we had to err on the side of caution and not drop our bombs. This policy was reinforced by the 1st MARDIV's JAG, who visited Al Asad six days prior to the war kicking off, and put the fear of God into us over friendly fire incidents.

'Following a series of civilian deaths in Afghanistan in OEF due to bombs hitting the wrong targets, the RoE in OIF was significantly tightened up in order to avoid a repeat performance in Iraq. You had to do a collateral damage estimate and have positive ID of your target before you could release your ordnance. This RoE applied whether you were firing your gun or dropping a 2000-lb bomb.

'During the briefing the JAG told us in no uncertain terms that if we screwed up, and they could get information to this effect fast enough, the investigation into the incident would have started before we had even landed back at base. We paid close attention to the briefing, and it was because of this that we did not drop our bombs on the first night of OIF.

Capt Ed Bahret (left) and his CO, Lt Col Michael Kennedy, pose with their BLU-109-toting F/A-18D at Al Jaber on 25 March 2003. Bahret flew two missions on this date, crewing up with his squadron boss on the second of these sorties. He recorded brief details pertaining to the flight in the following diary entry;

'25 March 2003/Call-sign "Epson 53"/OIF/Target – ammunition storage facility. Paired up with my commanding officer, we led a flight of two Hornets to drop a total of six JDAM. Flight went as planned. These flights were sometimes not very exciting since we drop these bombs from very high altitudes, sometimes over 40,000 ft, while simply flying over the target, before exiting the area and going home – much like a heavy bomber of World War 2. However, we were told that the secondary explosions at the target went on for more than five minutes as Iraqi ordnance cooked off inside the storage bunkers. Not a bad day, two combat flights, six large bombs off my aircraft and not a scratch' (*Capt Ed Bahret*)

'The combination of a confusing battlefield, poor weather and obsolescent targeting systems on our jet meant that I could not positively ID the targets, or provide a collateral damage estimate, after making several runs over them at 5000 ft. The same applied to the CO's section, which also returned without dropping any ordnance.'

According to VMFA(AW)-533 WSO Capt Doug Glover, the JAG's briefing was put into an OIF mission context by I MEF's Lt Gen Conway;

'When he came to MAG-11 and spoke to us directly, the thrust of his message was, "If you shoot first, then Collateral Damage is the issue. If the enemy shoots first, Proportional Response is the issue". Lt Gen Conway made it clear in no uncertain terms that if the enemy placed equipment near mosques, homes, schools and hospitals, and then used that equipment against Marines, we were to destroy it immediately with a proportional amount of force. Unfortunately, more often than not what aircrew remembered were the implied threats from the JAG, instead of the direct authorisation to engage the enemy from the I MEF Commanding General. In my opinion, misunderstandings about the RoE drove many aviators to be too cautious in the opening days of OIF, until our noses were bloodied at An Nasiriyah and the gloves came off.'

The restrictive RoE observed in the early stages of the campaign were frustrating for the crews involved, as the Marines on the ground certainly needed their help as they pushed into Iraq. Amongst those 1st MARDIV troops seeking the help of TACAIR was FAC Capt Brian Foster;

'I was in action from the very start of the war, crossing the border on the first night soon after Safwan Hill had been attacked and the berms breached. We went into Iraq without any planned air support, instead relying on MAG-11 jets manning ground alert CAS or TACAIR assets holding overhead in CAS stacks, waiting to be called into action.

'The war started a little early for us, and we had to call in some jets that were already in Iraq flying other missions to support our push across the border. Their ordnance was not set for our requirements of course, and they showed up with load-outs bearing no relation to what we had requested! With the weather being so bad, we ended up not using TACAIR. It was left to the main battle tanks to take out the RPGs and the handful of T-55s that we encountered as we entered enemy territory.

'Weather conditions were poor, with visibility down to less than a mile in places because of a sandstorm. We relied on thermal nightsights to see if there was any kind of heat signature coming from the tracked vehicles, and even if there wasn't, the tank still got destroyed.

'I tried to get some of the jets in the area to descend below the weather in order to check out the battlefield ahead of us. The most difficult part of the war for the infantry was the reduced line-of-sight, as there is no terrain to get up on top of in the south. Therefore, wherever possible, I got fast jet crews to tell us what lay ahead. That was particularly important when working with tanks, for the range firing advantages of the Abrams over Iraqi T-55s and T-72s was worthless if you could not see your enemy until you were on top of him. We used air support a lot in this role – particularly so on that first night of the war – in order to get eyes out in front us so as to see what was out there.

'The sandstorm limited the TACAIR jets' ability to reconnoitre the battlefield on the 20th, as although the sky was clear above 5000 ft, it was

Hornet pilot Capt Brian Foster swapped his F/A-18C for an M1A1 Abrams during OIF, the latter serving him well during his time in Iraq as a FAC with Bravo Company, 2nd Battalion, 5th Marine Regiment;

'I strapped my radio receiver to the top of my Abrams and duly joined its three-man crew, which left no room inside the tank for a FAC-dedicated radio operator once my gear had been stowed. I was left to run the radios on my own. My company was comprised of 12 tanks in total, and I was the sole FAC. Bravo Company 2nd Tanks was the only tank company attached to an infantry battalion. There were three infantry line companies in the battalion, the latter numbering 1200 soldiers. Typically, the Marines had two FACs and an air officer for every three line companies. This meant that there were usually two FACs up front with the troops.

'I controlled a total of 72 sections of aircraft during OIF, and of those, about 30 actually dropped or fired ordnance for me. Virtually every one of these strikers was talked onto a target by me from my tank. I would be head-out of the turret, scouring the landscape for landmarks that could act as target markers. You are only ten feet above the ground in the turret of an Abrams, so your field-of-view is limited. I always felt exposed when spotting for targets, and I was regularly fired at. Indeed, the tank next to mine was hit by an RPG during one attack – it was just 25 metres to our right. An RPG has virtually no effect on an Abrams, however. We were also struck many times by machine gun fire' (*USMC*)

weathered in below this height. Two of the Hornet crews I was trying to get information from came down to 3000 ft – inside the MANPAD MEZ (missile exclusion zone) – but they could not find a break in the cloud.'

Capt Charles Dockery of VMFA(AW)-121 also found himself caught up in the general confusion that marked the stuttering start of MAG-11's OIF campaign on 20 March;

'That afternoon my pilot and I were tasked with flying the unit's first FAC(A) mission of OIF. Two hours prior to our take off we had no information on what we were supposed to do, where we were supposed to go, what our call-sign was and who we were meant to talk to once in Iraq! We suited up and walked out to the flightline, and it was whilst en route to the jet that we found out that I MEF had commenced its penetration of the berm defending the southern Iraqi border.

'We strapped into our jet at 1945 hrs and waited on the tarmac for the next four hours for the order to launch. By the time we were told to go, we had a call-sign and we knew that we were going to help support the Marines on the ground. We launched as a single ship and headed north, and once over Iraq we found that the situation was chaotic. Indeed, the people controlling TACAIR assets on scene were the aircrew themselves, vice the controlling agencies on the ground. There were jets everywhere, and it was up to the crews themselves to control the chaos and keep everyone moving in one direction.

'We had bare bones information when we launched, and were lacking crucial instructions such as was there a tanker airborne, and if so, where was it and what was its frequency and call-sign? I was surprised at how chaotic things were on that first night, as despite months of planning, the response to the missile attacks took everyone at MAG-11 by surprise.'

The poor command and control exercised by the 3rd MAW's TACC caused much frustration amongst TACAIR assets during the opening 72 hours of OIF, as Capt Dockery mentioned. Col Jeffrey White was one of four battle captains who ran the TACC, and he was on-shift when the attack on Safwan Hill was ordered;

'We went from having 48 hours to get ready to go, to having four hours to get ready to go. For the first two days the TACC operated at less than optimal rhythm, with issues such as transitioning to the wartime ATO and Battle Damage Assessment (BDA) reports taking some time to catch

MAG-11's two F/A-18C units got through a lot of 'dumb' bombs whilst working over the various regular Army and Republican Guard divisions ranged against I MEF in eastern Iraq. This VMFA-232 jet (BuNo 163722) has been armed up with three 1000-lb Mk 83 bombs beneath its left wing, two of which are affixed to a BRU-33 Canted Vertical Ejector Rack. The aircraft also has a solitary GBU-16B/B LGB attached to the outer starboard wing pylon. VMFA-232 flew the most sorties of any MAG-11 unit, whilst maintaining the highest mission-capable rating of 90 per cent – despite flying the oldest Hornets at Al Jaber (*VMFA-232*)

Strewn with the detritus of a shattered army, this kill box in southern Iraq was typical of the areas repeatedly worked over by MAG-11 Hornet crews in OIF. Note the holed bunker in the centre of the photograph, and the numerous revetments (*Capt Ed Bahret*)

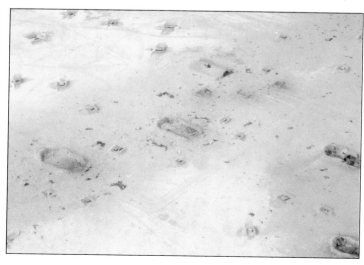

up with the troops' advance on the ground. By 23 March the TACC had turned the corner. The Marine Corps and the Army had started OIF on the enemy's timeline. We didn't have time to do the battlefield shaping that we would have preferred. Weather also hampered our ability to shape the battlefield too. For three days the system was constipated. By the 23rd the weather had cleared and systems began to fully operate on the war ATO – 80 per cent battlefield shaping and 20 per cent CAS.'

Capt Dockery concurred with Col White, telling the author;

'After stumbling into action on 20 March, by day four, the DASC (Direct Air Support Center, run by the Marines Corps) and the TACC had caught up with the war, and everything then ran like clockwork when it came to target assignment. I was definitely afraid pre-war that our ground command and control of TACAIR was going to be identical to the hell we experienced every time we conducted a Combined Arms Exercise (CAX) at Twenty-Nine Palms, in California. With CAX, we always seemed to be dealing with the youngest, most inexperienced controllers in the Marine Corps. For OIF, I think that the "A-team" was drafted in to run the DASC.'

CONTROLLING THE BATTLEFIELD

Having rapidly seized the Rumaylah oilfields, I MEF pushed north along Highway 8 towards An Nasiriyah, defeating the Iraqi Army's 51st Mechanised and 11th Infantry Divisions along the way thanks to the CAS support of MAG-11. This pattern of rapid advance was made possible through the concentrated firepower that the five Hornet units, supported by Marine Corps AV-8Bs and RAF Tornado GR 4 and Harrier GR 7s, could bring to bear through close control by F/A-18D FAC(A) crews.

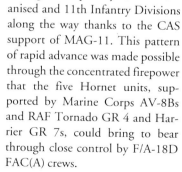

Much thought had gone in to how best to control TACAIR assets in OIF once the ground war got into full swing, with Gen Tommy Franks challenging his war planners to integrate as many air assets as they could into an overall network of 'joint fires' that directly supported ground force commanders heading north. CENTCOM staffers duly employed the Fire Support Coordination Line (FSCL) concept, which delineated a moving line up to which the 'joint fire' assets – jets, attack helicopters and artillery – were under the control of ground force commanders in the field, and beyond which they fell under the jurisdiction of the Joint Forces Air Component Commander (JFACC), or in MAG-11's case, the TACC and/or the DASC.

Anyone could engage targets that were positively identified as enemy military units beyond the FSCL without real-time coordination with ground units, while targets short of the FSCL had to be coordinated with the ground commander in whose area of responsibility (AOR) the target was situated. The kill box system, detailed later in this chapter, was used to make the process of updating the FSCL easier, as it allowed the latter to rapidly change without the reissuing of coordinates defining the line.

This was a radical plan, as traditionally all TACAIR strikers had been controlled exclusively by the JFACC in a time of conflict. Gen Franks placed even more faith in his senior officers on the ground by opting for a 'deep FCSL' once the invasion commenced, this seeing V Corps and I MEF divisional commanders controlling all 'joint fires' out to 100 miles. The value of this extended FCSL was quickly realised when the rapid advance north saw friendly forces crossing the 'joint fire' line. Had CAS-committed TACAIR assets been controlled by the JFACC only, then the potential for friendly fire incidents could have been huge due to AWACS controllers not being fully aware of how far ground forces had advanced.

In an effort to allow the JFACC to also play its part in the 'deep FCSL' strategy, CENTCOM relied on the tried and tested kill box system. This saw a ground commander split up his area of responsibility into 18.5-mile x 18.5-mile boxes, which he would then declare 'closed' when his troops entered them. Such a system shifted the 'joint fires' responsibility from the JFACC to the ground commander, thus reducing the chance of 'blue-on-blue' fratricide. When a kill box was declared 'open', the JFACC would assume that it was clear of friendly forces, thus allowing Coalition TACAIR to prosecute enemy targets.

The F/A-18D, manned by a FAC(A)-qualified crew, quickly became the 'go to' asset in OIF when it came to running open kill boxes. Performing the SCAR (Strike Coordination and Reconnaissance) mission, MAG-11 F/A-18Ds would cycle back and forth from the tanker to the kill box, providing ongoing control and marshalling other strike assets expeditiously into areas where they had located targets. Effectively operating as the scouts in a hunter-killer team with other TACAIR assets ranging in size from battlefield helicopters to B-52s, FAC(A) crews would converge on enemy targets well forward of the Coalition frontline and run air strikes against them for hours on end.

Kill Box Inderdiction, CAS and SCAR quickly became the key MAG-11 missions as V Corps and I MEF pushed north, with both forces deliberately manoeuvring around strong points in towns such as An Nasiriyah, Al Kut and An Najaf in an effort to get to Baghdad as quickly as possible in true *Blitzkrieg* style. Air power was the chosen means of keeping these pockets of resistance holed up in the southern and central towns and cities while Coalition forces headed north at rapid speed.

The kill boxes opened up a fixed area that was usually short of the FSCL for the attack of targets without coordination with ground units. As I MEF and V Corps moved northward, the FSCLs marched north with them. Kill boxes were opened on their flanks, where no friendly forces remained, to allow air power to eliminate threats in these vulnerable areas.

Beyond the FCSL, the TACC and/or the DASC continued to 'shape the battlefield' in advance of the mechanised troops through the CAOC-controlled, pre-planned battlefield air interdiction (BAI) sorties. Fixed, or limited mobility, targets hit during these missions included troop concentrations held in reserve, reveted armour around Baghdad and the selective destruction of bridges so as to stop Republican Guard forces south of the Iraqi capital retreating into the city itself.

One of VMFA(AW)-121's FAC(A)s was Capt Charles Dockery, who explained to the author how such missions were usually run in OIF;

'Prior to launching on a typical OIF FAC(A) sortie, my pilot and I would briefly sit down in the ready tent and look at the current ground scheme of manoeuvre in order to work out the two places where we would most likely be asked to perform the FAC(A) and CAS missions. We would also take ATARS imagery as a back-up in case we were pushed somewhere else to perform SCAR.

'Other than this pre-mission preparation, which ensured you had primary and back-up CAS areas to work, and a similar set up for SCAR, there was no point in spending hours preparing for a sortie, as you could be tasked to go and work virtually anywhere in central and southern Iraq. If that was the case, and you were sent to work in the middle of nowhere, you had to fall back on local knowledge of the area and your maps.

'We were only specifically tasked to work with ground forces prior to take-off on two or three occasions at most. The most memorable of these was when my section was told to provide aerial cover for 3rd Battalion, 1st Marines, which was staging a raid into the town of Ash Shatrah, north of An Nasiriyah. The Iraqis had captured a Marine from one of the many supply routes that ran through the area, killed him and then paraded his body through the streets of the town. 3-1 Marines was going in to retrieve the body at night, and we were pulled aside soon after arriving in the ready tent and given brief details of the plan.

'They were looking for four specific buildings to be destroyed before the battalion was sent in, and because these were in a built-up area, my pilot and I had to do some collateral damage estimates. With the latter in mind, we shifted our target run-in headings around and figured out precisely where we were going to lase the buildings for our bombs. LGBs have a tendency to fall short, so we had to shift our directions of attack around to ensure that if they did indeed do this, they would only impact in an open field and not strike a nearby house. When we showed up overhead, none of the targets had been hit. We razed one to the ground and then brought in a CAS section to destroy the rest.

'On a more typical FAC(A) mission, you would fly into Iraq and immediately check in with the TACC, followed by the DASC. Either of these organisations could hand you over to one of the air officers assigned to an RCT in the frontline, and if they had no trade, you would instead be assigned an open kill box by the DASC. Hopefully, the kill box that you were given was one of those that you had planned to attack as a standby target if there was no direct-action CAS available. If this was indeed the case, then you would break out your imagery and start identifying target locations prior to reaching the kill box.

'If there was already someone working in this area, you would conduct a quick sitrep handover and then go looking for targets. If we were the first into the kill box, then we would immediately start checking out our imagery-identified target areas to see if these had been recently worked over. Once we had a list of valid targets, we would work down the day's ATO in search of TACAIR assets in our area. We usually had an idea of who we would be working with prior to them showing up.

'MAG-11 soon worked out that the best way to run the KI/CAS mission was to send the FAC(A)-crewed jets out from Al Jaber 15 minutes ahead of three to four staggered sections of CAS players. If you got pushed to a ground unit once on-station then great, but if not, then you were assigned a kill box to control and the FAC(A) jet would turn into a SCAR platform. You would immediately start finding targets for the TACAIR jets coming up behind you at 10-15 minute intervals.

'By arriving early, you would have targets ready and waiting for when the first section checked in. Once in radio contact, I would tell the Hornet or Harrier II pilots, "Here is your target, here is how I want you to attack it, here are your run-in headings and here is how I want you to pull off the target". Once those guys started working, you then moved onto the next target, and so the pattern was repeated until you had either hit everything within your assigned area, or you had exhausted your fuel and handed the kill box over to another FAC(A) crew.'

TIME-SENSITIVE TARGETS

Although working with a FAC(A) crew greatly helped single-seat Hornet pilots to get their bombs off quickly before their jets went fuel-critical,

A FAC(A)-crewed F/A-18D from VMFA(AW)-533 prepares to get priority gas ahead of a section of LGB-toting F-14Ds from VF-2 on the morning of 2 April 2003. All five Tomcat units involved in OIF also had a number of FAC(A)-qualified crews within their number, and they did sterling work over Iraq too. In fact the D-model F-14 was perhaps the ultimate FAC(A) platform during the conflict, as it had excellent endurance, a great targeting pod, a handy bombload and reliable radios. The only downside for the Tomcat was the distance the jet had to travel to reach Iraq from the NAG or the eastern Mediterranean (*Maj Doug Glover*)

Amongst the more colourful Hornets to see action in OIF was VMFA(AW)-533's F/A-18D BuNo 164959 (*Maj Doug Glover*)

Although not used as much as in *Desert Storm*, the CBU-99 still regularly featured in the mission load-out of MAG-11 Hornets during OIF. Each cluster bomb unit was filled with 247 Mk 118 Mod 0 bomblets, and these proved deadly when used against troop concentrations, reveted artillery and soft-skinned vehicles. These 'personalised' CBU-99s have been up-loaded onto a BRU-33 attached to the starboard outer wing pylon of a VMFA(AW)-225 F/A-18D (*Capt Ed Bahret*)

Three F/A-18Cs from VMFA-251 prepare for a division launch (the photographer – an RAAF pilot on exchange – is flying the fourth jet) from Al Jaber (*VMFA-251*)

a fair percentage of the missions flown by VMFA-232 and -251 consisted simply of two-ship sections servicing target coordinates given to them by the TACC, the DASC or FACs. Air strikes on TSTs by MAG-11 assets were also often flown by single-seat jets independently of FAC(A)s, as the following after action report from VMFA-251 illustrates;

'On 24 March 2003, a flight of two F/A-18Cs flown by Capts "Dung" Bailey and "Quatto" Gallagher launched on a night mission from Al Jaber. Initially, they were not given specific tasking, and tanked twice before being contacted by "Tropical" – the real-time Targeting Cell in the TACC. "Tropical" passed a coordinate for a surface-to-surface missile (SSM) battery near Basra that was preparing to shoot Al Samoud missiles into Kuwait.

'The pilots proceeded overhead the coordinates and began searching for the vehicles. The two SSM launchers were discovered along the side of a road, with support vehicles in the vicinity. One of the SSM launchers was elevated in preparation to fire, so the pilots quickly set up for an attack. Capt Bailey targeted the northern launcher with his CBU-99s and Capt Gallagher hit the southern one with his cluster bomb units.

'Capt Bailey's CBUs opened properly, spreading bomblets across the launcher and destroying it. Capt Gallagher's CBUs did not function properly, detonating without opening once they impacted near the southern launcher. Capt Bailey quickly called for his wingman to follow him through the target area, expending both aircrafts' Mk 83s on the southern launcher, destroying it as well.'

Such TST missions provided a welcome diversion from the endless SCAR and CAS sorties flown by MAG-11, as the CO of VMFA-232, Lt Col Mike Burt, explained to the author;

'In a break from CAS and SCAR, which were our "bread and butter" missions in OIF, we were given a TST to hit in Basra just as we checked into the operations tent. We ran to our jets, jumped in and took off. It was a short mission, as Iraq was only 60 miles from Al Jaber, and Basra was 30 miles further north from the border. We worked with a SOF FAC embedded in the city itself, who told us when we checked in with him, "You are cleared hot on the target that you were briefed on". We duly dropped our JDAM on a seven-storey building that was the HQ for the special presidential police in Basra and then returned home.

'The TST missions were always neat, as haste was the order of the day with them. A SOF operative had usually spotted a key regime target entering a building, and he had made the call that this location had to be hit ASAP. These missions were typically given to the alert crew – we always had two pilots suited up ready to run to their aircraft, which were bombed and fuelled up on the ramp. We would get the call, with the frequency to check into and the grid reference to hit, and off we went.'

Lt Col Burt and his pilots understood that although TST missions were important for the overall war effort, their daily KI/CAS, SCAR and BAI sorties had more of a direct bearing on their Marine Corps brethren pushing north to Baghdad. One of the key targets that they were regularly sent against during these missions was artillery, which the Iraqis seemingly had no shortage of. Lt Col Burt told the author;

'We had a target priority list that saw us going after things that would hurt the Marines the most as they pushed north. At the top of this list was artillery, which Saddam's forces had plenty of. Anything that remotely resembled an artillery piece in the field had to be taken out as quickly as possible after it was found. This point was drummed into us by the division commander during a briefing he gave at Al Jaber pre-war. His parting words were, "If there is anything you can do for me, then get rid of that artillery, as that will save Marines' lives on the battlefield.

'Artillery pieces were hard to spot in OIF, particularly with our NITE Hawk FLIR, which was not as good as some of the other targeting pods in-theatre. I spent many a night staring at the cockpit DDIs (Digital Display Indicators) over the target area trying to break out exactly what it was I was looking at through the pod. Fortunately, for much of the war we had the luxury of being able to orbit over a target-rich area trying to ID aim points without being too worried about SAMs or AAA. The latter was always present right up until war's end, but we negated its effect by staying above it. Occasionally, larger calibre 105 mm shells would be seen, and these usually detonated above us.

'We knew that the Iraqis weren't tracking their rounds, however, as we had no indication on our RWR (radar warning receiver) gear that there were any fire control radar systems active. It was simply barrage AAA, which posed little threat to us as long as we stayed at around 15,000 ft.'

'KILLING MACHINE'

Much of MAG-11's best work was done against the regular Army and Republican Guard divisions charged with defending the cities of An Nasiriyah, Al Amarah, As Samawah and Al Kut. The sheer number of targets destroyed by Marine Corps jets during this critical phase of OIF in late March and early April provoked the following response from I MEF's

Lt Gen Conway when questioned by a journalist post-war about why the campaign fought by the Marine Corps had been so successful in Iraq;

'The power of I MEF made a real difference to the outcome of the war. We had this outfit called the 3rd MAW, and I will tell you, frankly, it's a killing machine.'

Word of how good the MAG-11 FAC(A) crews had become in the 'Hunter-Killer' role quickly spread to the USAF, as Lt Col Burt recalled;

'Stories about the effectiveness of our Marine Corps FAC(A)s soon made their way over to the Air Force and Navy units in OIF, and they were desperate to come and work targets on our side of Iraq. Once the fixed targets of "Shock and Awe" had been exhausted by the Air Force and Navy, they looked to the Army for additional CAS and SCAR tasking, and discovered that they were not using a whole lot of TACAIR to support their advance – they preferred to use artillery and main battle tanks, as well as the occasional Apache strike. The Air Force and Navy strikers therefore pushed to get into the Marine Corps game, as we had dropped a fair amount of ordnance on a whole host of targets. Although we may not have been bombing key strategic regime targets, we had been helping to shape the battlefield by knocking out artillery and the like so that it could not be used against our Marines on the ground.'

Indeed, USAF pilots were so keen to work with the FAC(A)s that they would regularly press them for future mission details at Al Jaber. VMFA(AW)-533 WSO Capt Doug Glover recalled;

'I had A-10 "drivers" I knew on base come up to me in the mess hall in order to find out when I'd be up as a FAC(A), and what kill box I'd be running, so that they would know where to fly to after working with the Army to employ the rest of their ordnance!'

The arrival of additional strike assets on the Marine Corps side of Iraq placed an additional burden on the already hard-pressed FAC(A) crews, as VMFA(AW)-121's Capt Charles Dockery recounted;

'Our FAC(A) missions got more involved with the arrival of the Air Force assets from the Army side. On a typical mission, we were assigned to work with three Marine Corps sections from Al Jaber, and possibly a Navy section or two, but from the middle of the war onwards Air Force jets started to flow in too. Working all these dissimilar assets proved to be quite a challenge. It was great that they were coming over expressly to work with us, but it made the job very difficult when you were trying to manage up to ten sections in one kill box.

'On more than one occasion I remember looking down at all the notes I had scrawled on my chart during the course of the mission and asking myself, "now where did I tell that guy to go?" It was a challenge, but I think the Marine Corps FAC(A) crews were up to it. Indeed, I only sent one section back home without dropping its ordnance – two A-10s showed up, and their elderly Pave Penny laser spot trackers which were used to locate our coded target-designating laser energy for their LGBs were unable to find our spot. I had aircraft backed up with better sensors which could locate my laser energy, so I had to send them home.'

Squadronmate Maj Jeff Ertwine also worked regularly with the Air Force, and he rated the F-15E crews that he controlled very highly;

'I loved it when Strike Eagles checked in, because they were just "wall-to-wall" with LGBs. They would typically show up with ten 500-lb

GBU-12s on each aeroplane, and towards the end of the war I began to struggle to find enough targets for them to hit!

'The F-15E crews were not technically supposed to be striking Marine Corps targets, as they were assigned to work with the Army. However, several Strike Eagle crews told me post-war that they would deliberately save fuel, but tell the Army that they were out of gas and heading home, and then check in with the F/A-18D FAC(A)s with 15 to 30 minutes of available loiter time. They knew that we would be able to make good use of their remaining bombs in a far more expeditious fashion than the Army FACs. They weren't used to the way the Marine Corps guided TACAIR directly on to targets, as the control they were familiar with usually consisted of a basic brief that went something like "That is your area – bomb over there"! By contrast, we were in there flying literally alongside them, telling them where the target was and what we wanted hit.'

This kind of talk-on control was desperately needed when running the target-rich kill boxes that proliferated around Al Amarah and Al Kut. FAC(A) crews tried to operate in section strength during this period simply because of the sheer number of aim points that required servicing, but this could not always be achieved due to the the mission tempo. Maj Ertwine and his WSO, Maj Mike Waterman, were forced to run a particularly chaotic kill box near Al Amarah on their own, as the former explained to the author;

'Usually, you would be able to hand over the running of an open kill box to a new FAC(A) crew just prior to heading out with bingo fuel to the closest tanker. This was not always the case, however, and on one such mission, when we were tasked with finding targets in a kill box near Al Amarah, we spotted a huge tank park just as we had to leave for fuel. The DASC cleared us to hit the target, but we told them that we were going off station and heading for the tanker. We told them that we would

The MAG-11 Hornets shared ramp space at Al Jaber with USAF TACAIR types from the 332nd Air Expeditionary Group, the RAF's Nos 1(F) and IV(AC) Sqns (the latter both equipped with Harrier GR 7s) and the AV-8B Harrier IIs of VMA-214. This formation photograph, taken just days after major hostilities had ended, is led by an A-10A of the Michigan Air National Guard's 172nd FS (five of the six OA/A-10A units committed to OIF were based at Al Jaber). To the A-10's right is an F/A-18C from VMFA-251 and a No 1(F) Sqn Harrier GR 7, whilst to its left is one of eighteen 524th FS F-16CGs that called Al Jaber home, and an AV-8B+ from VMA-214. The latter unit was the only permanently land-based Marine Corps Harrier II squadron of OIF. Behind the formation can be seen MAG-11's TACAIR ramp. Note that all of the aircraft are carrying live ordnance (*Capt Ed Bahret*)

be back in the kill box in about 30 minutes, and that they could start sending jets there in anticipation of our return.

'A section of A-10s was the first on scene, and they tried to control the flow of jets in. All of a sudden it was like ants to a picnic, and I could hear all the calls on the radio as we sat behind the tanker. I told my WSO that I almost didn't want to head back to the kill box, as I knew that confusion was reigning without a dedicated FAC(A) on scene.

'As soon as we came off the tanker, the DASC ordered us straight back to the kill box. I immediately instructed my WSO that we had to take control of the airspace and get these guys into a CAS stack, as they were all over the place. As a FAC(A) crew, that was our job in OIF – stacking

VMFA(AW)-225 ATARS jet BuNo 165531 joins the end of the queue behind a Marine Corps KC-130T on 1 April 2003. Sandwiched between it and the tanker are two F/A-18Cs from VMFA-251 and four AV-8Bs. Note the F/A-18D's 'Willie-Pete' rocket tubes which are fully loaded (*Capt Ed Bahret*)

Capt Ed Bahret took this photograph whilst working over a kill box near Al Kut on 2 April 2003 (*Capt Ed Bahret*)

TACAIR from 15,000 ft up to 31,000 ft, and running strikes on targets in an orderly, organised fashion. We had ten sections working this kill box, and we were positioned below the lowest section at just under 15,000 ft.

'Our first customers were two RAF Harrier GR 7s, and they experienced trouble identifying the target we had given them, so we marked it with rockets. They came back around on their attack runs, but they were still baulking at our ID. We had 18 jets stacked up behind them, so I told the RAF guys in no uncertain terms that they had one more pass at the target, and if their RoE did not allow them to ID it to their satisfaction then they had to clear the area for the strikers behind them who might be able to acquire the aim points with their sensors. They made one more pass but were not happy with their target ID so they left without expending their ordnance.

'A section of A-10s was next on scene, and I told them, "You have three passes to get rid of everything, and then proceed ten miles south and egress as we don't want you back". They were followed by a section of Hornets with LMAVs (AGM-65E laser Maverick missiles), but no operable lasers to guide them! This meant that I had to rendezvous with the lead jet, bring him in and then lase the target for his weapon. I then repeated the routine for the Dash-2 jet. Both jets had two LMAVs apiece, and I buddy-lased different targets for each and every one of them. I then turned my attention to the next section, marking a target for them and telling them that they had two passes to get all their bombs off. By this time the next FAC(A) crew was checking in, and we told them to go up to 33,000 ft and wait for the handover.

'This sortie was typical of the missions that we flew throughout OIF. It was our job to enter an open kill box and impose order on the TACAIR assets that were literally falling over themselves to attack a target. We had to take the crazed chaos and create order so that as many of the targets would be serviced effectively in the short time that the kill box was open.'

With the forces of the Iraq Army's 6th and 10th Armoured Divisions and the 14th and 18th Infantry Divisions having been worked over by MAG-11 day in and day out along Highway 8 from the very start of OIF, by 1 April these formations posed no threat to I MEF's right flank as the Marine Corps turned its attention to Al Kut.

Maj Ertwine was heavily involved in this pivotal stage of the campaign;

'We worked targets around Al Kut for three days solid from 1 April, which was the longest we operated in a single area during the entire war. TACAIR took on and eradicated the Baghdad Division of the Republican Guard, and I got to control B-52s, B-1s and all manner of smaller fighter-bombers during this period. CENTCOM used MAG-11 as a manoeuvring unit during this phase of the war, the ATO telling all TACAIR units at Al Jaber that our sole mission for 72 hours was the annihilation of the Baghdad Division. And that is exactly what we did.

'In the wake of the aerial offensive, the 1st Marines then drove north along Highway 7 out of An Nasiriyah to engage the Baghdad Division in Al Kut, and the 5th and 7th Marines headed around to the northwest and then circled back to the east through An Numaniyah, before crossing the Tigris and also heading right for Al Kut. 7th Marines committed first to the fight with the Baghdad Division, and 5th Marines was to follow, but after a several small firefights around a palm grove, the enemy just gave up. So instead of the 5th Marines turning right, they turned left and headed for Baghdad. TACAIR had been almost exclusively responsible for defeating the Iraqi Republican Guard's largest division.

'During the aerial battle of Al Kut, our squadron had three FAC(A)s airborne simultaneously – one east of the Tigris, one west and a third over a huge ammunition depot. We had staggered our launches by about 45 minutes, but we were all airborne for around six hours, so our times on station overlapped considerably. We divided the FAC(A) target sections amongst the three of us, and we all worked the same frequency. As sections checked in for targets, we pushed them to whichever FAC(A) had the capacity to handle their ordnance at the time. The trio of FAC(A) crews worked targets with sections of single-seat MAG-11 Hornets for four hours solid. The division of the target areas by the Tigris also made the controlling of TACAIR assets that much easier for us, as the strikers used the river as a visual reference point when it came to locating targets.

'We also controlled the B-52s that were brought in to help bolster the firepower on call. They would simply check in as they approached Al Kut, perform a ten- to twelve-mile run in as they got set up and then drop their ordnance against grid coordinates given to them by us. I tried to join up with them once but only got close enough to see the bomb-bay doors open up. I did not see the bombs themselves falling away. The B-52 crews appreciated the speed and efficiency synonymous with operating on the I MEF side, vice the red tape of the Army and Air Force set-up in the west.'

Having dealt with the Baghdad Infantry Division of the Republican Guard, MAG-11 turned its attention to the elite Al Nida Armoured Division, protecting the eastern approaches to Baghdad. Again, it was left to TACAIR to attrite the dug-in Iraqi positions, and with targets becoming more and more difficult to find, Hornet crews experienced some hairy moments as USAF elements came east 'freelancing' for trade. VMFA-232's Capt Byron Sullivan recalled;

'Our management of kill boxes during the Al Nida Division massacre worked well up to the point when the Air Force showed up. They would monitor the radios and listen out for where the targets were, and then come in to our areas looking to drop their bombs. They were usually operating on a different frequency, so you couldn't talk to them. All of a sudden there would be all these other aircraft in your kill box running amok! I remember rolling in on a target, ready to pickle my bomb, and an F-16 flew right across the nose of my jet.'

Squadronmate Capt Justin Knox was similarly unimpressed by how the TACAIR war was being waged in the last ten days of OIF;

'Things really started getting hairy towards the end of the war, when everyone was desperate to drop their ordnance on a dwindling number of targets. Guys began radio frequency hopping if they could not get a target allocation on their assigned frequency. Once this started happening, you had no idea who was working on what frequency, and with whom, and you could not talk to them. There were a lot of cowboys in the area who weren't following the correct procedures as laid down by the CAOC. Things got so bad in the last few days over Tikrit that my main concern was not AAA or SAMs, but the mid-air threat posed by Coalition aircraft.'

And it was not just USAF fast jets that posed problems for MAG-11 crews, as VMFA(AW)-225's Capt Ed Bahret explained to the author;

'I was never scared by the enemy's SAMs or AAA, but once we started hitting the Al Nida Division east of Baghdad I became greatly concerned that we were going to be involved in a mid-air collision with either another Coalition aircraft, or ordnance dropped by a TACAIR asset. Everyone wanted to work over the same targets in the same piece of ground as the battlefield shrunk in the final week of the war.

'Our close shave came in early April when my wingman and I were conducting a gentle diving LGB attack on tanks in the open. Closing on the target, our formation was bisected by two objects heading for the ground. Fortunately, we had some separation in the formation, with our wingman providing cover and generally scoping the area as we ran in on the tanks – we could not believe that this was such a permissive environment, so we maintained our standard look out as we had been trained to do. Two MAG-13 Harriers had come into the area from the opposite direction to us, and their superior Litening targeting pods had managed to ID the tanks at a greater distance than our NITE Hawk sensor. This meant that they could get their bombs off in double quick time. The Harrier pilots never saw us, and the objects we spotted falling between us were their LGBs!'

URBAN CAS

With the Republican Guard divisions defending the southern and eastern suburbs of Baghdad obliterated by TACAIR, I MEF's RCTs 1, 5 and 7 commenced the final phase of OIF on 7 April when they started to push into the Iraqi capital. MAG-11 aircrew had long feared how they would stand up to the task of providing CAS support for friendly forces in an urban environment. They were fully aware of how difficult this was going to be, and their targeting abilities were tested as they tried to walk the fine line between supporting troops under fire, 'danger close', on the ground and obeying the strike RoE that applied to operating in urban areas.

Three days prior to the assault on central Baghdad, VMFA-232's Capt Byron Sullivan had had his first taste of urban CAS while helping a Marine Corps convoy that was searching for a safe spot at which to cross the Tigris River, before pressing into the city itself;

'I was flying with the Operations Officer of MAG-11, Lt Col Kevin 'Wolfy' Iiams – he had survived a SAM strike in a VMFA-451 Hornet during *Desert Storm*. Whilst on the tanker, I asked a FAC(A) crew that were also topping off their tanks whether there was any action going. They mentioned that a Hornet FAC called "Fingers" that we knew had just been ambushed near Baghdad.

'Having got our fuel, we headed directly to the ambushed convoy and dialled up the FAC (not "Fingers"). We could hear things blowing up and the troops taking rounds, and shortly afterwards the FAC we were talking too went silent – his vehicle had received a direct hit. The convoy was

MAG-11 Hornet units rarely flew in mixed formations during OIF simply because it was easier for squadrons to work up their own flight schedules independently of one another. Indeed, this photograph of a JDAM-armed VMFA(AW)-533 jet patrolling Iraq with an LGB-toting VMFA(AW)-225 machine was taken several days after OIF I had ended on 20 April 2003. All five Hornet units at Al Jaber worked their jets hard during the war, and aside from targeting pod gripes and poor ATARS reliability, the aircraft coped just fine with the increased 'op tempo' according Maj Jeff Ertwine of VMFA(AW)-121;

'We flew the crap out of our jets, yet they stood up to the mission tempo incredibly well. We had all the parts we needed, and all the personnel required to keep the jets airworthy. The aircraft held up really well overall. Our full mission-capable rate was around 92 per cent for our fleet of 12 aircraft, 11 of which we flew regularly – like most units, we had one airframe that we robbed for parts throughout OIF.

'The only areas where we could improve the F/A-18D in terms of mission suitability would be to equip it with a better targeting pod – which is now happening with the Litening pod – and increase the jet's endurance. And the two are interlinked, for if we had a better pod, then we could successfully acquire targets more quickly, thus saving precious fuel when on-station. A lot of our time, and therefore fuel, was wasted simply trying to find targets in OIF' (*Capt Ed Bahret*)

Baghdad proved to be a magnet for camera-toting Hornet aircrew conducting post-war patrols of Iraq. The city suburbs and the snaking Tigris River form an impressive backdrop for VMFA-232's F/A-18C BuNo 163495 on 22 April 2003. Two weeks earlier, this jet was involved in the fight to seize the Iraqi capital, although like all other Hornet units in-theatre, VMFA-232's ability to perform urban CAS was seriously affected by its total reliance on the antiquated and unreliable NITE Hawk pod. Squadron pilot Capt Heath Reed lamented;

'Undoubtedly the biggest drawback for us in the legacy Hornet during OIF was our inability to identify targets with our FLIR pod. The other strikers in-theatre – the Harrier IIs, the Tomcats and the Strike Eagles – all had better pods with superior magnification that allowed their pilots to identify targets from altitudes above the MEZ. We had to rely on visual acquisition with our eyes, or through binoculars – I found the latter to be too big and bulky in the cockpit, and I was always banging them into the frigging canopy!

'The only time we used our pod was for target designation when it came to the delivery of LGBs. During daylight missions, we would lock up the target with the pod using coordinates provided by the FAC/FAC(A) after first acquiring the aim point with our eyes. Confirming this with the FAC/FAC(A), we would lase the target and drop our LGBs. At night, using NVGs, the target resolution for identification was no better than using the NITE Hawk pod' (VMFA-232)

being shelled by artillery that was less than a mile away, hidden alongside a large road. The Iraqis had just lit the large oil trenches that surrounded the city, and the convoy was also being hit by RPGs fired at close range by troops masked by smoke blowing through the area.

'Having lost our first FAC, we got in touch with "Fingers", who could see where the artillery was coming from. He managed to count up the number of pieces that were attacking them, and give us good coordinates.

'I had a vanilla pod on my jet, which meant that the FLIR had no operable laser for guiding LGBs onto the target. In truth, the FLIR in the NITE Hawk often worked so poorly anyway that I rarely used it. I preferred to look out of the cockpit and see what was going on, endeavouring to lock up the target visually whenever possible.

'I quickly spotted the Iraqi troops along the oil trench line, and also the artillery muzzle flashes "three smoke stacks up", as "Fingers" had told me over the radio. By now a FAC(A)-crewed F/A-18D had also arrived on the scene, and we started working with it. The FAC(A)s could not find the target, and the pilot got on the radio and asked me what I was looking at the artillery pieces with. I replied, "My fucking eyeballs, and I'm rolling in from the south!" "Wolfy" and I hit two of the artillery pieces with our 1000-lb Mk 83 slick bombs, which were too big to employ near the Marine Corps convoy – this weapon's blast radius is about half-a-mile.

'Our attack stopped the shelling, but the Marines were still being hit with RPGs and small arms fire, which had knocked out vehicles at either end of their convoy. This meant that wounded troops could not be evacuated for treatment by road, so they called for a Medevac helicopter. Initially, the area was deemed to be too hot for it to land, so my section and the FAC(A) Hornet were cleared to conduct strafing runs – the friendlies were too close for bombs to be dropped. We had to descend to 2000 ft in order to spot the enemy troops prior to opening fire on them.

'The following day, a squadronmate of mine also did some strafing in support of an ambushed Army convoy in northern Baghdad. His target was a ubiquitous white pick-up truck – we saw these all the time in OIF. The Hornet pilot could hear the FAC taking fire but could not see any targets. He radioed the FAC, "All I can see is a bunch of white trucks", and was told in reply "SHOOT EVERY FUCKING WHITE TRUCK. EVERY FUCKING WHITE TRUCK IS HOSTILE!" We knew that these things were being used by the bad guys, despite the vehicles lacking any distinguishing military markings.

'I well remember spotting a concealed tank under a bridge on Highway 7 and being in the process of rolling in on it when three white Nissan pick-ups stopped alongside it and the tank crew bailed out of their MBT and fled in these vehicles! I asked my controller whether I could drop on the white trucks and was emphatically told NO! I swear that every person in Iraq owned a white truck. The enemy was not stupid when it came to the employment of these ostensibly commercial vehicles, loading them up with Fedayeen fighters and ammunition and using them to re-supply defensive positions virtually at will, day or night. It was virtually impossible to make a visual ID on those damn things, and they literally had to be shooting at your guys before you were cleared to engage them without the possibility of getting your ass fried post-mission.'

As US forces began to seize control of Baghdad, a concerted effort was made by CENTCOM to eradicate high value leadership targets before they could be spirited out of the city. At the top of the list was Saddam Hussein himself, and VMFA-232's Lt Col Mike Burt was involved in one of the last decapitation sorties aimed at eliminating the Iraqi President;

'On 7 April I was involved in the B-1 JDAM strike on the restaurant in the al-Mansour district of southwest Baghdad following intelligence that Saddam Hussein was dining in this establishment with this sons Uday and Qusay. My wingman and I were up on CAP with the B-1, and I could see him about 20 miles to the east of us. We were both performing a standard CAS mission, working with the same SOF guy on the ground.

'He came up on the radio with a coordinate for my wingman and I to hit after he confirmed that we had four JDAM between us to drop. I knew straight off the bat that he was SOF, as he briefed the attack differently to how I was used to. He was laid back about the whole deal, passing me the grid coordinates and then asking me to read them back as per standard operational procedure – I read them back once I had typed them into the jet's mission computer. He replied, "Affirmative, you are good to go".

'There was undercast across Baghdad that day, so I couldn't see the city, let alone the target. I plotted the coordinates on my map and discovered that my aim point was right in the centre of downtown Baghdad, on the banks of the Tigris. This made me very nervous! I radioed the FAC once more to confirm this was where he wanted our bombs, and he replied, "Sure thing. Bring it on!", so we pickled a solitary bomb each and pushed out of the area. I could still see the B-1 nearby throughout this time.

'About a minute later the SOF guy got on the radio and said, "That sounded great! Can you do it again?" I replied in the affirmative, and he adjusted the coordinates a little bit, prior to us releasing our remaining JDAM. Once again he was effusive about the accuracy of our dropping. Having expended all of our ordnance, we bid him farewell and headed back to Al Jaber. Once on the ground, I made a point of heading straight to our operations tent and typing the coordinates of the target into our computer-stored file of satellite imagery. When I blew up the relevant photograph on the screen I was astonished to see that we had just bombed one of Saddam's monster palaces in central Baghdad.

'Two days later, I was flying over the same area again, and I dropped down to below 10,000 ft and made a couple of reconnaissance runs over the palaces. I could clearly see four huge holes punched through the domed roofs of the central building, with large craters beneath them.

'Within five minutes of us hitting the palace, the B-1 had dropped his JDAM on the restaurant, which was only five blocks away. I am not sure whether the two strikes were connected, with the SOF guys hedging their bets that he may have been at either of these locations – hence the fact that they were both hit one after the other. As it transpired, he was at neither.'

Forty-eight hours after the restaurant strike, Capt Charles Dockery of VMFA(AW)-121 was also involved in a Saddam-triggered incident that followed hot on the heels of an abortive urban CAS mission;

'In the pre-dawn hours of 9 April I flew my most frustrating mission of OIF. We were supporting RCT-5 as it entered Baghdad from the north, and then drove south towards one of Saddam's palaces. The taking of the latter was a key objective, along with other high value buildings known to house regime targets. My pilot on this occasion was Maj "Mel" Brooks.

'As soon as we arrived over the city, we got coordinates for the lead elements of the convoy. We watched them drive down a narrow road towards the palace, being attacked by small arms and tracer fire from both sides. I informed my pilot that I could not tell who was firing on who, which meant that there was no chance of us providing direct fire support without the risk of us inflicting casualties on friendly forces. We remained in orbit overhead, and I was in constant radio communication with the FAC, whose transmissions were being made against the background noise of high-intensity small arms fire. He was continually having to break off "comms" in order to "button back up" inside his tank because of the intensity of the enemy fire on his position.

'The road was too narrow for us to start slinging ordnance into the area, and although the FLIR allowed me to track the way the convoy was moving, I couldn't make out our troops on foot. We continued to act as frustrated observers overhead the RCT-5 convoy until it finally reached the palace at sunrise. The ordnance we were carrying was too big for what they wanted us to do with it, our 1000-lb LGB having too much of a footprint when detonated, and our unguided "Willie Pete" five-inch rockets not being accurate enough to hit small targets with precision.

'With the palace taken, 1-5 Battalion was told to head to the northwest of the city to seize a mosque on the banks of the Tigris where it was reported that Saddam was taking refuge. Again, we were overhead when this operation commenced, and the FAC asked us what we could see from our vantage point. We had two A-10s with us, and we stuck them 2000 ft below us so that they could scope the mosque with their laser seekers, and we were also working our FLIR and I was looking at streets in the area through my binoculars.

'Although I could see little activity around the mosque, as soon as the Marine-manned Armoured Amphibious Assault Vehicles pulled up outside, they immediately came under sustained small arms and RPG fire. I told the FAC where some of the RPGs were coming from, and offered to drop one of my LGBs into the building in "safe" mode – it simply became a 1000-lb

VMFA(AW)-225's distinctively marked colour jet (BuNo 165532) also made the flight north to Baghdad post-war. The unit's Capt Ed Bahret had seen plenty of action over the Iraqi capital in the final days of OIF I, including an unusual mission that he flew in support of the US Army's V Corps;

'Hours after ground troops entered Baghdad, my section had the privilege to work with the lead element of the Army's 3rd Infantry Division (ID). The latter had just reached Highway 8, on the southern outskirts of the Iraqi capital, as we got on-station, which meant that we had enough fuel to cover their movement into the airport. We covered their progress for 20 minutes, then had to head off-station to get more fuel, before returning to the battlefield.

'Whilst we were on the tanker one of the Army's Abrams was disabled by a lucky RPG shot in the middle of the highway, and rather than stop to recover the tank, the 3rd ID pushed on after attempting to knock it out with a grenade thrown through its hatch. The grenade failed to do much damage, and after the convoy had moved through, the Army asked us to target the tank for destruction. However, permission through the Army chain of command took so long that we never got to destroy the Abrams due to us reaching "bingo" fuel' (*Capt Ed Bahret*)

block of concrete. The FAC checked with the company commander and he said that they were too close for any air-dropped weapons, and that they would have to take the mosque room-by-room through hand-to-hand combat.

'Again we were left to watch the whole event unfolding below us, unable to influence its outcome.

'We then had to go to the tanker just as the Marines were entering the mosque, and when we came back the regimental air officer sent us across the Tigris to look for a target

that was inside the Army sector of control. He told us we were looking for ten Mercedes sedans, probably in a convoy. We soon found them, and I asked him what he wanted us to do? He replied that he was waiting for national command authority to attack them. We orbited overhead the target for a full 25 minutes but never got permission to hit the vehicles.'

With Baghdad effectively in Coalition hands by 10 April, MAG-11 turned its attention to the northern city of Tikrit, which was the final centre of Iraqi resistance. Lt Col Burt was amongst the Hornet pilots who dropped their last ordnance on targets in and around the city;

'Once V Corps and I MEF got into Baghdad, we weren't used that much any more because of collateral damage issues. In the main, Marine Corps Cobra gunships were left to conduct urban CAS because there were too many civilians in the city for us to be bombing enemy positions in the centre of residential areas. We were pushed north to work with Task Force *Tarawa*, which was given the job of capturing Tikrit – the last city to fall to the Coalition. By then we were exclusively destroying fixed targets identified by Marine Corps FACs and FAC(A)s – vehicles, tanks, ammo bunkers etc. – rather than providing CAS for troops in contact with the enemy. The latter had by now lost their appetite for the war.'

On 19 April MAG-11 Hornet units flew their final OIF I missions. During the 30 days of major hostilities, the five F/A-18 squadrons had flown more than 2700 of the 4000 KI/CAS, SCAR and BAI sorties undertaken by MAG-11. Averaging 120 to 130 flights a day during the campaign, the units had flown more than 500 sorties (1300+ flight hours) apiece, and dropped an accumulated total of 4.2 million pounds of ordnance by war's end. Much of this weaponry was expended on the ten regular Iraqi Army and two Republican Guard divisions that MAG-11 helped annihilate. But these statistics only tell part of the story. The final word on the effectiveness of MAG-11 in OIF should come from one of its principal customers – an unnamed RCT air officer who e-mailed his thanks to MAG-11's Operations Officer at Al Jaber on 22 April 2003;

'Hornets outshined all other air assets from my unbiased perspective. We used Hornets in situations where we would normally have preferred to use Cobras, and your guys pulled it off without a hitch. MAG-11 should be very proud of the outstanding support you provided us with.

'The Hornets were *always* there when we needed them.'

VMFA(AW)-121's aircrew and maintainers pose for an informal group shot at Al Jaber on 10 April 2003. The unit was awarded the prestigious Commandant's Aviation award for 2003 by the Marine Corps Aviation Association following near back-to-back operational deployments in the previous 12 months. Between 1 May 2002 and 30 April 2003, VMFA(AW)-121 amassed 1468 combat sorties (5495 combat flying hours) and dropped 861,949 lbs of ordnance during OEF, OSW and OIF operations. It is little wonder, therefore, that the unit achieved the 'best overall performance and accomplishment of all assigned tasks by a Marine Corps squadron' during this period (*VMFA(AW)-121*)

COLOUR PLATES

1

F/A-18A+ BuNo 163133 of VMFA-115, USS *Harry S Truman* (CVN-75),
Mediterranean Sea, April 2003

2

F/A-18A+ BuNo 163155 of VMFA-115, USS *Harry S Truman* (CVN-75), Mediterranean Sea, April 2003

3

F/A-18A+ BuNo 163133 of VMFA-115, USS *Harry S Truman* (CVN-75), NAG, December 2004

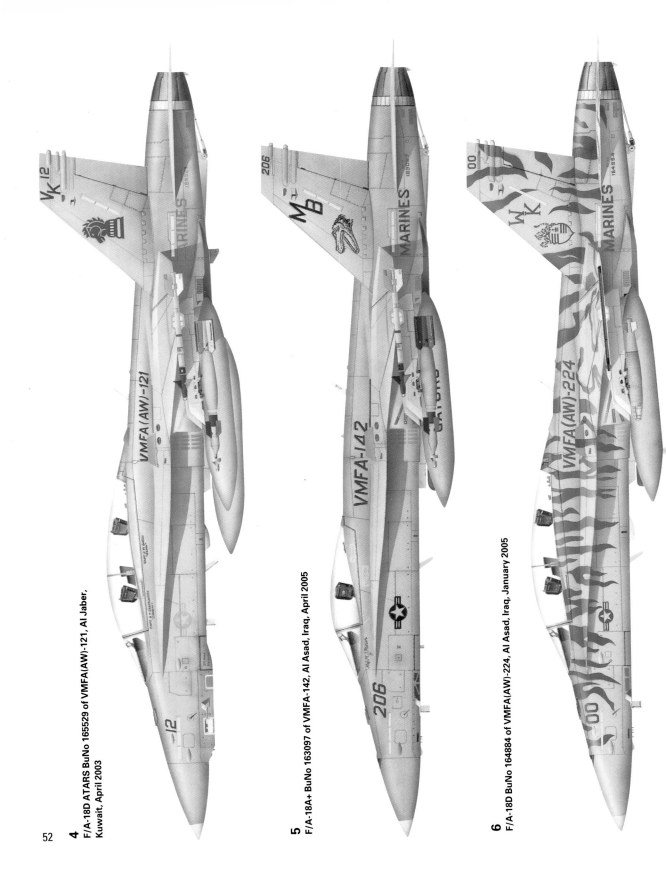

4
F/A-18D ATARS BuNo 165529 of VMFA(AW)-121, Al Jaber,
Kuwait, April 2003

5
F/A-18A+ BuNo 163097 of VMFA-142, Al Asad, Iraq, April 2005

6
F/A-18D BuNo 164884 of VMFA(AW)-224, Al Asad, Iraq, January 2005

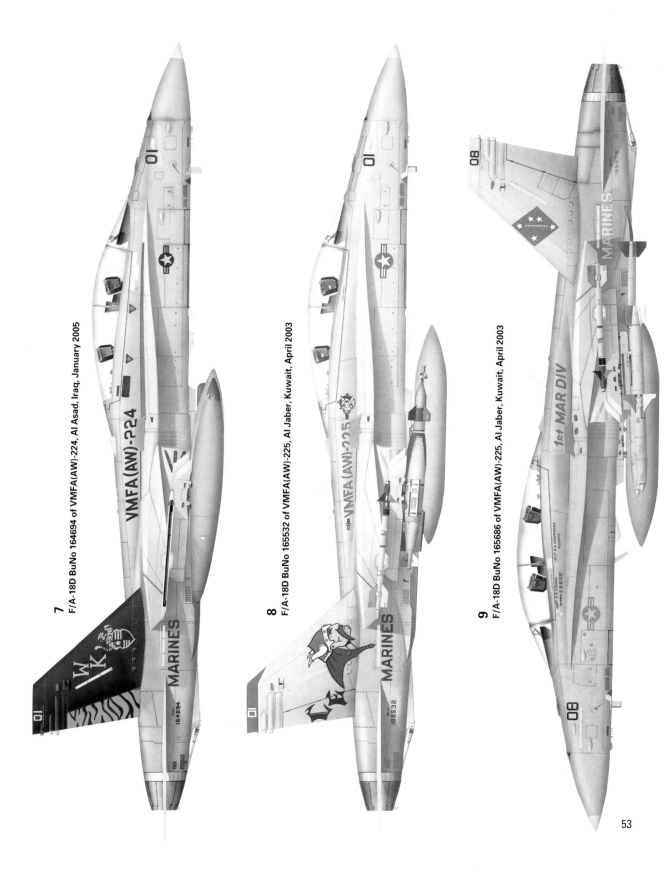

7
F/A-18D BuNo 164694 of VMFA(AW)-224, Al Asad, Iraq, January 2005

8
F/A-18D BuNo 165532 of VMFA(AW)-225, Al Jaber, Kuwait, April 2003

9
F/A-18D BuNo 165686 of VMFA(AW)-225, Al Jaber, Kuwait, April 2003

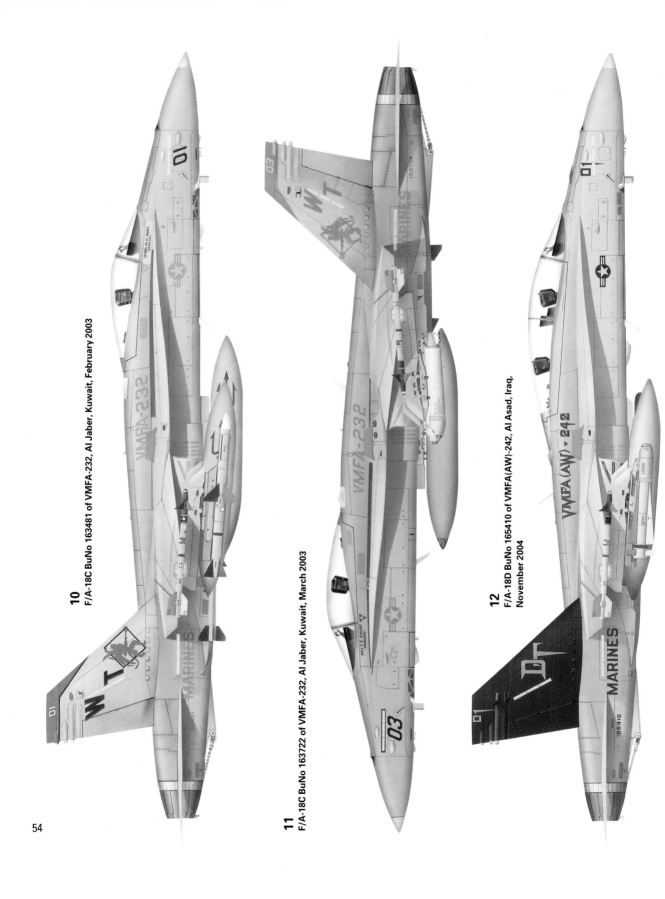

10
F/A-18C BuNo 163481 of VMFA-232, Al Jaber, Kuwait, February 2003

11
F/A-18C BuNo 163722 of VMFA-232, Al Jaber, Kuwait, March 2003

12
F/A-18D BuNo 165410 of VMFA(AW)-242, Al Asad, Iraq,
November 2004

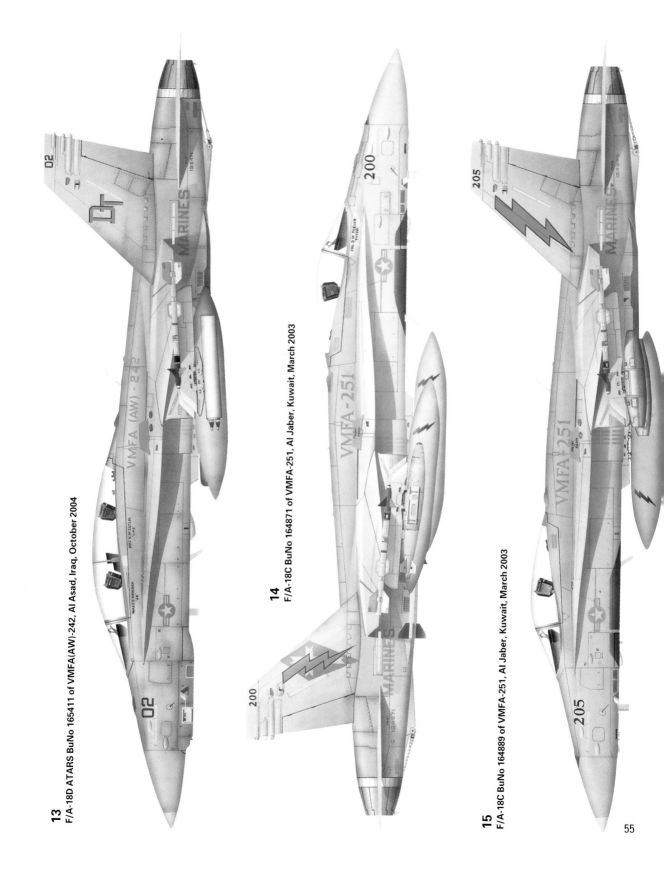

13
F/A-18D ATARS BuNo 165411 of VMFA(AW)-242, Al Asad, Iraq, October 2004

14
F/A-18C BuNo 164871 of VMFA-251, Al Jaber, Kuwait, March 2003

15
F/A-18C BuNo 164889 of VMFA-251, Al Jaber, Kuwait, March 2003

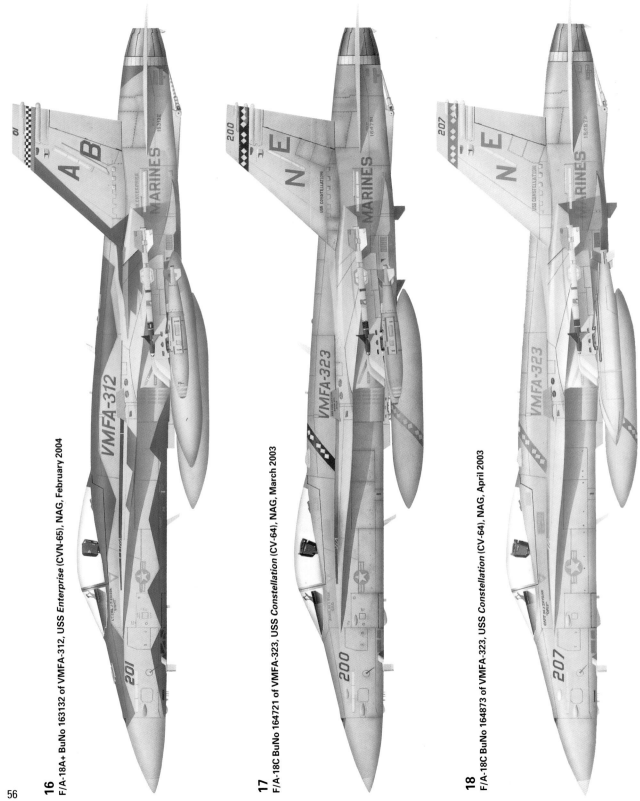

16
F/A-18A+ BuNo 163132 of VMFA-312, USS *Enterprise* (CVN-65), NAG, February 2004

17
F/A-18C BuNo 164721 of VMFA-323, USS *Constellation* (CV-64), NAG, March 2003

18
F/A-18C BuNo 164873 of VMFA-323, USS *Constellation* (CV-64), NAG, April 2003

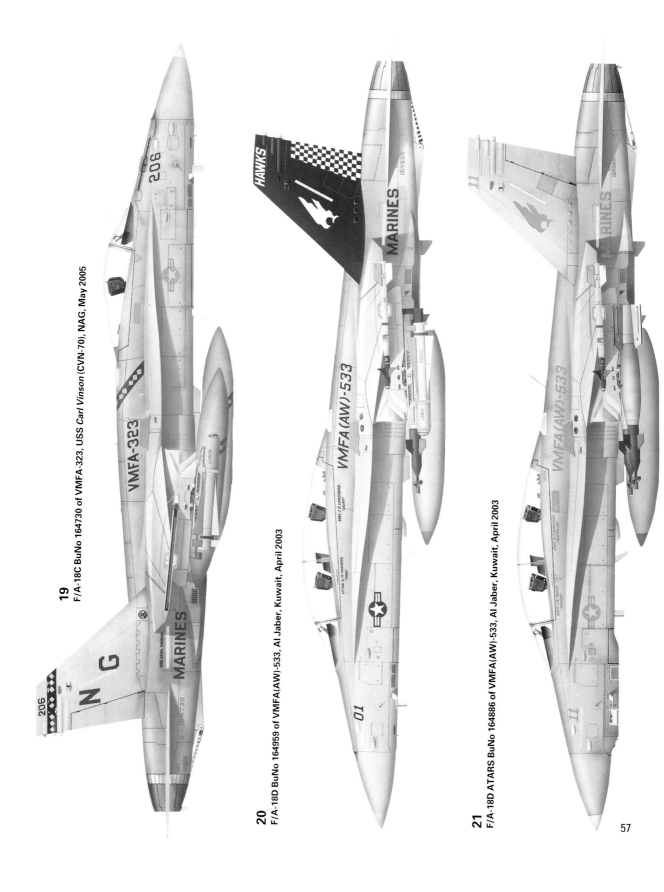

19
F/A-18C BuNo 164730 of VMFA-323, USS *Carl Vinson* (CVN-70), NAG, May 2005

20
F/A-18D BuNo 164959 of VMFA(AW)-533, Al Jaber, Kuwait, April 2003

21
F/A-18D ATARS BuNo 164886 of VMFA(AW)-533, Al Jaber, Kuwait, April 2003

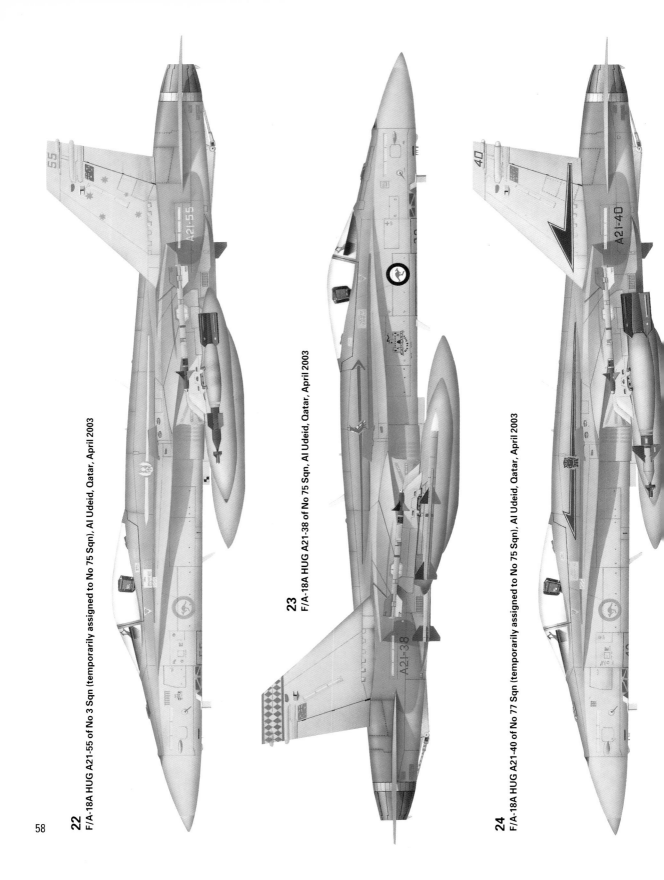

22
F/A-18A HUG A21-55 of No 3 Sqn (temporarily assigned to No 75 Sqn), Al Udeid, Qatar, April 2003

23
F/A-18A HUG A21-38 of No 75 Sqn, Al Udeid, Qatar, April 2003

24
F/A-18A HUG A21-40 of No 77 Sqn (temporarily assigned to No 75 Sqn), Al Udeid, Qatar, April 2003

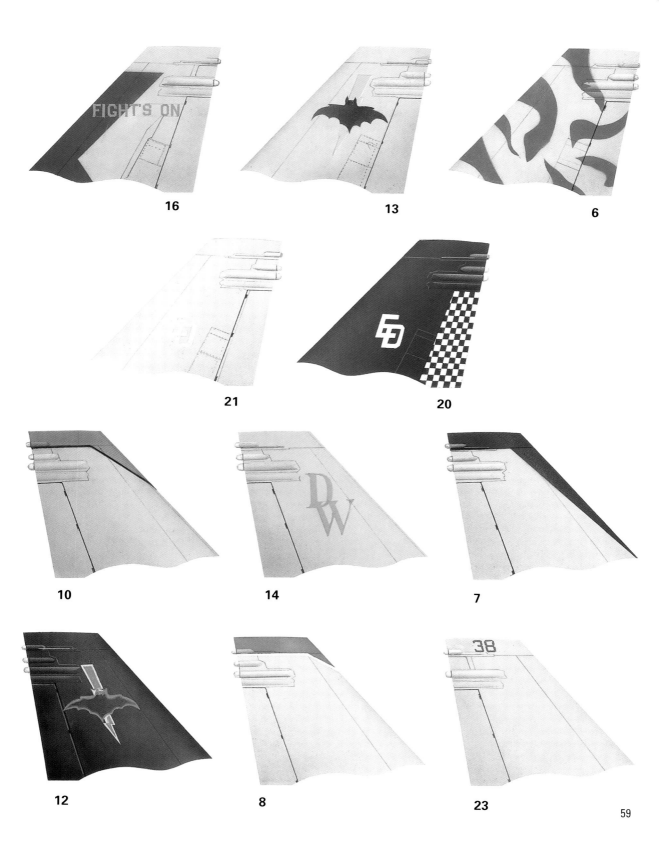

16

13

6

21

20

10

14

7

12

8

23

1

19

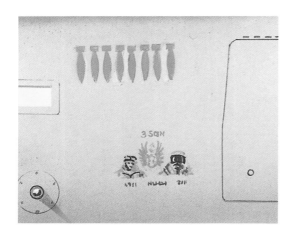

22

23

FROM THE SEA

For the two carrier-based Marine Corps light strike units involved in OIF, their air war was different, at least initially, to that fought by their MAG-11 brethren at Al Jaber. Both VMFA-323 in the NAG aboard CV-64 and VMFA-115 embarked in CVN-75 in the eastern Mediterranean would play significant roles in 'Shock and Awe', only turning their hand to the KI/CAS, SCAR and BAI missions that dominated OIF after the targets on the CAOC's ATO had been attacked.

As detailed in Chapter 2, the ground war started 24 hours before 'A-Day', and as with MAG-11, this caught VMFA-323 out. CVW-2 was still flying ATO-driven OSW missions when I MEF pushed through the berms into the Rumaylah oilfields. One of the flights launched just as this event was taking place included Capt Guy Ravey within its number;

'I was supposed to fly to Basra on the evening of 20 March as part of a division of Hornets (two each from VMFA-323 and VFA-137) on call for CAS for the Marines moving into Umm Qasr and the Rumaylah oilfields. The brief was standard, and, surprisingly, little mention was made to the fact that the war seemed to have actually kicked off, although this had not yet been officially confirmed. We manned up and prepared to launch just like a normal OSW mission, but just prior to departing the ship the Current Operations desk on CV-64 contacted us with target coordinates. Immediately, the adrenalin began to flow. We had a very compressed cycle time, so we needed to launch, get our gas and press out to the area as quickly as possible so that we could get our bombs off and recover.

'The ship was located in the central NAG, 180 miles from Kuwait, so it took 20 minutes to get up to the Kuwaiti coast. As we got closer to "feet dry", we could see the lights of Kuwait City and a low haze layer of dust and smoke. Underneath the gauzy blanket covering the battlefield, we started to make out the flashes of artillery, which made a momentary, nebulous glow and then disappeared. I had seen artillery before during exercises back in the US, so it didn't cause too much concern. The next thing I saw did, though.

'Northwest of Kuwait City, I saw a bright flash underneath the fog, followed by a bright point of light streaking skyward at an unbeliev-able rate of knots. "SAM launch!" I thought to myself. We were still 50 miles from the coast, but the flash didn't bode well to me. The missile was followed almost immediately by three other similar arcs of light. Estimating their altitude, I figured they were climbing well above 50,000 ft. As we got closer, I noticed that a faint finger of smoke trailed

VMFA-323 first cruise pilots Capts Guy Ravey (left) and Chris Collins (right) head for the ready room after completing their last OIF mission – an armed reconnaissance flight over Al Taqaddum – on 13 April 2003. Both men are wearing standard fast jet pilot garb, namely a g-suit, torso harness, survival vest, skull cap and helmet. Capt Ravey claims that he felt like an 'overstuffed Thanksgiving turkey' whenever out of the cockpit of his beloved Hornet in his flying apparel. Slung over the pilots' shoulders are their all-important helmet bags, the contents of which Capt Ravey explained to the author;

'The helmet bag is a green nylon sack (not a purse!) in which we *never* put our helmets, but do fill with all the charts, reference guides and other mission-essential items we need to complete our flight. During OIF I also threw in a peanut butter and jelly sandwich, four "piddle packs" for inflight bladder relief, a "camelback" water system to keep me hydrated, my 8 mm video tapes for recording mission data and a memory unit for insertion into the jet's mission computer. In all, my "man bag" weighed about 15 lbs when full' (*MSgt Timothy DuPont*)

behind each one, and the arcs actually headed north *towards* Iraq. It wasn't until we landed that we figured out the SAMs were actually Army Tactical Missile System rounds being launched against Iraqi positions.

'We checked in with our controller aboard an orbiting USAF AWACS platform, and I could tell the guy was obviously task-saturated. His voice was high-pitched and he missed numerous calls. This was to be my first true experience with the fog of war. We knew we only had 20 minutes of useful time on-station before we'd have to return to the ship for fuel considerations, yet the battlespace manager was content to leave us in a holding pattern directly over the battlefield while he tended to other business. He passed us off to another controlling agency, but we didn't have their frequency. It took us five minutes of yelling over the radio at the controller to finally get the frequency he wanted us to switch to.

'When we finally contacted the agency – the Marine DASC – he told us that he had no idea who we were, nor why we wanted to talk to him! We informed him that we had target coordinates, and were requesting permission to drop. "Not my call. Contact 'Karma' (the AWACS!) for clearance", he replied. We were pounding on our canopies in frustration. Here we were, four Hornets with bombs at our disposal and coordinates to drop on, holding over the battlefield, getting shot at, and we're playing phone tag with the controllers. The AWACS finally got so overwhelmed that he came up on clear frequency guard channel and passed, "All players, All players. If you are an interdiction player you are cleared to drop. All X-CAS and X-INT players need positive clearance to drop". That call didn't help us because we were on the schedule for "Attack".

'We tried again to get a word in edge-wise with "Karma", but he ignored all our calls. Finally, we agreed over the tactical frequency amongst ourselves that this was war, and they wouldn't have passed us those coordinates if they didn't want a bomb dropped on them. We set up for our runs with just enough fuel and time to get our bombs off and get home. My lead, Maj Pyle Gundlach, was five seconds away from pickling his JDAM when "Karma" finally asked us to contact him. A quick call was made but "Karma" didn't respond. We had to abort. How infuriating!

'Nobody said anything on the way home, save for one call made by Dash-4 – "What a fucking cluster-fuck!" We felt like we had missed the opportunity to really help out our Marines on the ground. We found out later that the "comms" problems got ironed out soon after we left, and our DMPIs were serviced by a later flight, but we still felt dejected. Three days would pass before I got the chance to remedy our first night fiasco.'

Looking every inch a war-weary warrior, 'Snake 201' (BuNo 164722) patrols over Baghdad on the morning of 17 April 2003. The numerous bridges that cross the Tigris in Baghdad can be clearly seen below the Hornet. One of these was the scene of a memorable urban CAS mission involving VMFA-323's CO. Capt Ravey recalled;

'Lt Col Thomas and Capt Taylor knocked out the approach road to one of the main bridges in northern Baghdad on 8 April during the seizing of the city, this attack being ordered in an effort to disperse Iraqi armour that was opposing the Coalition advance. Both Hornet pilots were flying with a mix of GBU-12s and GBU-35s, which were fitted with fuses that required at least 20 seconds of flight to arm them. They ended up rolling in on the target, as that was the only way they could achieve an accurate laser designation for the weapons that would avoid the bridge itself being hit by mistake. The pilots managed to get a JDAM into vehicles on the western side of the bridge, followed by a GBU-12 that detonated amongst some dismounted enemy troops. This attack stopped the Iraqi incursion across the bridge' (*VMFA-323*)

Some 24 hours later VMFA-323 played a key part in the opening Baghdad strike of the 'Shock and Awe' campaign, as the official war diary of the unit's CO, Lt Col Gary Thomas, detailed;

'Lt Col Thomas was the alternate Mission Commander for the first strike by Coalition aircraft in support of OIF. As the primary planner for strike package OBS, he orchestrated the attacks of 68 coalition aircraft against 91 targets in and around Baghdad. The target set included leadership, command and control, air defence and offensive strike assets. The package consisted of 20 F/A-18s, 8 F-14s, 10 EA-6Bs, 8 F-15Es, 7 F-117s, 3 B-2s, 8 F-16CJs and 4 Tornado GR 4s. Flying as Dash-3 in the Mission Commander's division (led by CVW-2 CO, Capt Mark Fox), they were tasked with destroying Al Samoud missiles in northwest Baghdad. Each aircraft was armed with three JSOW. Post-mission analysis confirmed the destruction of the Al Samoud missiles.'

Lt Col Thomas' boss, Capt Fox, explained to the author what CVW-2 and VMFA-323 were trying to achieve on 'A-Day' of 'Shock and Awe';

'The opening strike – consisting of multiple salvos of cruise missiles and Coalition strike aircraft – targeted hundreds of aim points in several sequential waves, making the first hours of OIF the most overwhelming delivery of precision ordnance ever seen. Designed to saturate and destroy Iraqi air defences, roll back the Baghdad SuperMEZ, destroy command and control nodes and degrade the ground forces' ability to defend Baghdad, the opening strike was impressive for a single evening's work.'

Follow-up strikes against fixed targets as far north as the Iraqi capital were the order of the day for VMFA-323 for the next ten days, with highlights including the one and only firing of an $874,000 AGM-84H SLAM-ER by an aircraft from CVW-2. Launched on 22 March against an LP-23 radar sited at Saddam International Airport, on the southern outskirts if Baghdad, it was one of only two AGM-84s expended in OIF.

Operating from the designated night carrier, and therefore conducting virtually all of their missions during the hours of darkness, the 18 pilots of VMFA-323 flew 152 sorties between 21 March and 1 April – 20 on 29 March alone. JDAM was the main weapon used during this phase of the campaign, with 30 2000-lb GBU-31s, 11 2000-lb BLU-109 penetrators, 42 1000-lb GBU-32/35s and 25 JSOW being expended. Targets hit included Al Samoud missile sites, Special Republican Guard barracks, Presidential Security buildings, ammunition bunkers, Iraqi Information Ministry communications facilities, Iraqi television HQ, leadership targets in the Radwaniyah Al Faris Club, the Baqubah, Balad Ruz and As Suwayrah military cable repeaters and radio relay facilities, the Latifiya satellite communication radio facility and a US Army AH-64 Apache that had forced landed in enemy territory.

Most of these targets were to be found deep within the Iraqi capital, which was well defended by the legendary Baghdad SuperMEZ.

VMFA-323's 'Snake 204' (BuNo 164727) departs CV-64's waist catapult on the eve of OIF, an AGM-84H SLAM-ER attached to its left outer wing pylon. This fixed target, precision strike air-launched missile saw very little use during the conflict. Indeed, only two SLAM-ERs were fired in anger in OIF, one by CVW-14's VFA-113 (on 22 March) and the other by VMFA-323. The latter unit fired its AGM-84H in the early hours of 22 March during the first 'Shock and Awe' strikes, Capt Nate Miller (in 'Snake 211' BuNo 164733, call-sign 'Stew 16') successfully targeting an LP-23 radar at Saddam International Airport. Although all three of *Constellation's* Hornet units had been trained to use the SLAM-ER, VMFA-323 was chosen to employ the weapon for real following experience it had gained during mission planning for a still-born AGM-84 operation that had been on the cards towards the end of OSW. Capt Guy Ravey recalled;

'With IrAF incursions on the increase in early March, CVW-2, and VMFA-323 in particular, received tasking from the CAOC to formulate a plan whereby a SLAM-ER attack would be mounted against the MiG-25s at either Al Asad or Balad Southeast. What stalled the operation was the lack of rock solid intelligence on the exact location of these aircraft, as CENTCOM was leery about the collateral damage issues relating to the million dollar SLAM-ER should the weapon have missed its intended target and hit something else' (*US Navy*)

Undeterred, VMFA-323, in conjunction with other CVW-2 assets, hit target after target as the CAOC ATO was diligently worked through. A typical mission for this period, flown on the night of 25 March, was described as follows in Lt Col Thomas' war diary;

'Capt W R Barber acted as a wingman on a TST strike ordered by President Bush. Having completed the briefing for their original strike mission, they received last minute re-tasking to strike Iraqi Information Ministry "comms" facilities in the heart of Baghdad. Capt Barber and his wingman began their detailed planning as they walked to their jets on the flightdeck. They were forced to complete the last of the coordination and strike planning airborne, to include arranging for SEAD coverage and manually entering the precise target coordinates in each of their weapons.

'Five targets in downtown Baghdad, spread over a five-mile area, were serviced with six BLU-109 JDAM 2000-lb penetrator weapons. Each target was located in a densely cluttered urban environment, and required extremely restrictive delivery headings to minimise potential collateral damage. The precise nature and high-profile of the targets struck is underscored by the fact that the "comms" facility was across the street from hundreds of foreign journalists staying in the Al Rasheed Hotel.

'Although initial Bomb Hit Assessment was impossible due to weather, open-source reporting from news agencies confirmed the destruction of the Iraqi Information Ministry's broadcast facilities, thus disabling its propaganda activities for several hours. This was accomplished with no collateral damage to the adjacent structures.'

CAS TASKING

Although VMFA-323 had flown a handful of KI/CAS missions against the 1st Hammurabi Division south of Baghdad on 30 March, the unit – and CVW-2 as a whole – began serious battlefield operations with V Corps from 1 April onwards. Capt Ravey explained to the author the procedures involved when tasked with performing such missions;

'We shifted operations from fixed strikes to CAS at the beginning of April, targeting Iraqi armour and troops around Karbala and Basra. The battle of Al Kut also started to heat up at this point. Indeed, I was airborne when RCT-5 rolled into Al Kut on 2/3 April. Maj M D Hawkins and I were over the town just as the sun was rising, and although our guys needed our bombs, we were not cleared to drop them. This was very frustrating, as the battlefield set-up lent itself to a classic CAS strike.

'There were bad guys on the north side of the river and good guys to the south, but everything was so congested in the town itself that we could

Bathed in early evening light and armed with a 1000-lb GBU-35 JDAM on its port outer wing pylon and a 500-lb GBU-12 LGB on its starboard inner pylon, F/A-18C BuNo 164873, flown by squadron XO Lt Col J R Woods, heads for Baghdad on 4 April 2003. Operating with the callsign 'Switch 07', Woods expended both of his bombs against revetted vehicles found on the outskirts of the Iraqi capital. Other targets hit on this day included a third vehicle, two revetted artillery pieces, a tank and a possible surface-to-surface missile site. A total of five GBU-35s and three GBU-12s were dropped, and all the targets serviced were located in and around Baghdad. VMFA-323 spent more time operating in this area than any other Marine Corps unit in OIF, and squadron pilots such as Capt Guy Ravey remained fearful of Baghdad's SuperMEZ until war's end;

'The Iraqi capital was heavily defended by SAMs and AAA throughout the campaign, with a large number of missiles being sited near a helicopter base in the southern sector of the city. The SuperMEZ blanketed Baghdad, which meant that the AAA and SAM sites were really concentrated right across the city. This meant that you had to have your wits about you whilst circling the target in preparation for the attack. Once the decision was made to go in and drop your ordnance, you were always protected by a Prowler and F-16CJs, both of which were HARM-equipped. Thanks to the EW threat posed by the latter assets, I never saw a guided SAM shot. We also kept height on our side too in order to defeat the AAA. We could make attack runs at altitudes of up to 30,000-35,000 ft thanks to the GPS accuracy of the JDAM (*VMFA-323*)

not pick out targets with any confidence. We had no FAC(A) present, and the guys on the ground were telling us little more than "there are enemy tanks coming south across a bridge, but I don't want you to blow up the bridge"! There was nothing more that we could do, short of circling over Al Kut. We were not permitted to go any lower in order to break out targets due to the MANPAD and AAA threat.

'Although it was frustrating not to get our bombs off, we knew that the troops would not be short of support, as there was a CAS stack 20,000 ft high waiting to be called in. Indeed, we saw an RAF Harrier GR 7 come in and drop an LGB on Al Kut just prior to us leaving the scene.

'Working the CAS stack in a Hornet took some doing, and you regularly returned home with more than 30 frequencies written on your kneeboard. You had to actively seek out target tasking during your brief time on station, and that meant running the radios through the various control agencies as you frantically sought permission to drop. We would talk to guys on "Have Quick" or "Crypto", depending on their location.

'The Marine Corps worked the CAS mission much better than the Army or Air Force, as it would push targets up to the highest level, which usually meant that we would be given a target as soon as we checked in on station. The guys running the DASC, and the FACs in-theatre, were also very savvy with the needs of a TACAIR pilot, as they were in the main ex-Hornet or Harrier II guys. This was never the case with the Air Force and Army FACs. If you arrived on station with JDAM, for example, a typical Marine FAC response to your request for a target would go along the lines of "I don't care who you are, but if you have a JDAM then these are the coordinates – go bomb the target. You are cleared to engage".

'The AOR was broken up vertically through the middle of Iraq, with the Marine Corps controlling the eastern side of the country and the Army and Air Force dealing with aircraft working in the west. The former had the TACC in place to run the TACAIR aspects of the campaign.

'The top level of the TACC was basically a check in/check out facility, whose call-sign was "Tropical". As soon as you went "feet dry" over enemy territory, you would check in with the "Tropical" controller, telling him that you wanted to work targets in eastern Iraq. Acting as the clearing-house for TACAIR, "Tropical" operated from a series of command and control-modified HUMVEEs, AAV7A1s and LAVs travelling north with I MEF. Although they periodically established base just behind the frontline, the "Tropical" team remained highly mobile, leapfrogging north as I MEF advanced on Baghdad. The TACC controller would then hand you off to the DASC, which was a level down in the "Tropical" chain. From there you would be given instructions to go and talk with Marine FACs working at the very tip of the I MEF spear.

'The Marine Corps also had a mobile DASC(A) set up in a KC-130T, orbiting near the FSCL. This was housed in a trailer that was shoehorned into the back of the Hercules. These guys were given the responsibility of filling in the target acquisition gaps when ground-based "Tropical" could not gain line-of-sight with the target, or was out of radio contact/range of the TACAIR assets on-station. The DASC(A), call-sign "Sky Chief", which was the forward eyes for DASCs "Chieftain" and "Blacklist", was subordinate to "Tropical" – the DASC is always subordinate to the TACC. The Marine Corps simply cobbled together what would work

best for it in OIF, and the "Tropical"/"Sky Chief" set up functioned well.

'"Sky Chief" remained on-station for hours at a time, orbiting on a very fuel-efficient profile over enemy territory. They had a terrific line-of-sight on the battlefield, being effectively a low-earth satellite when on-station. They could talk with all of the Marine Corps units on the ground, relaying target coordinates to TACAIR crews orbiting overhead.

'Unlike their Army and Air Force brethren, the TACC/DASC controllers would actively seek you out in order to find you targets to hit. They would be up front with you, stating right off the bat whether there was anything going on in their battlespace. The Air Force, on the other hand, often seemed too overwhelmed by the sheer number of TACAIR assets in-theatre to deal with individual pilots seeking targets to bomb. They also seemed to lack an understanding of the Hornet's capabilities, as we were regularly asked to go and ID vehicles on their behalf with our virtually useless NITE Hawk pod, as the Air Force controllers thought that our pod was as capable as the F-15E's vastly superior LANTIRN.'

Having operated over Baghdad for much of OIF, VMFA-323 flew a number of urban CAS missions supporting US forces as they entered the Iraqi capital during the second week of April. The unit's attention then turned to Tikrit, where, on 14 April, a section of two Hornets launched on a strike/CAS mission were tasked with hitting several L-29 Delfin and L-39 Albatros jet trainers at a nearby airfield that were suspected of having been modified to act as nuclear/biological/chemical weapons delivery platforms. Each pilot dropped a single 500-lb GBU-12 LGB into the line of aircraft, scoring direct hits. Three days later, with major hostilities now over, CV-64 was relieved in the NAG by USS *Nimitz* (CVN-68) and 'Connie' departed the Arabian Gulf bound for home.

VMFA-323's missions statistics for OIF make for impressive reading. The unit's 12 F/A-18Cs flew 262 sorties (842.6 flying hours) between 20 March and 15 April, and during that time they expended 319,272 lbs of ordnance. The latter figure was comprised of 67 500-lb GBU-12s, eight 1000-lb GBU-16s, 96 1000-lb GBU-32/35s, 41 2000-lb GBU-31s, 23 2000-lb BLU-109 penetrators, one 500-lb Mk 82 'dumb'

Some 22 of the 36 F/A-18Cs assigned to CVW-2's trio of Hornet units during CV-64's OSW/OIF war cruise crowd *Constellation's* bow on 15 April 2003. VMFA-323 had dropped its final ordnance of OIF, near Tikrit, 24 hours earlier. Mission details are provided by the following entry from the CO's war diary;

'Capt Peterson and Lt Cdr Rauch (CVW-2 staff officer) launched on a strike/CAS mission and were eventually tasked with hitting L-29 and L-39 jet training aircraft that were suspected of being modified as nuclear/biological/chemical delivery platforms. Each pilot expended a GBU-12 LGB and scored hits. Both targets appeared to be destroyed.'

Later that day a section of jets was tasked with bombing a nearby ammunition bunker, although only one pilot dropped a single GBU-35 on the target after his wingman's JDAM hung on the pylon. Capt Ravey had a GBU-31 hang on 24 March, and here he explains the procedure for getting rid of it;

'If a JDAM hangs you have to wait 20 minutes before you can jettison it. This is because the thermal battery which powers its guidance system is activated when you hit the release switch in the cockpit. If you jettison the bomb before the battery power has run out, it will still attempt to make it to the GPS coordinates programmed into its guidance system, even thought there is no way ballistically that it can do so' (*VMFA-323*)

bomb, one AGM-65 LMAV and one AGM-84 SLAM-ER. Some 1368 rounds of 20 mm ammunition had also been fired. The total value of all this ordnance was a cool $11,082,353.07!

WAR IN THE NORTH

Just as confusion reigned in the south on 20 March following the accelerated start to OIF, things were no clearer for the sole Marine Corps Hornet unit assigned to Carrier Task Force 60 (CTF-60) in the eastern Mediterranean. As I MEF

JDAM came into its own in the early days of OIF in the north, when bad weather meant that only fixed targets could be attacked by CTF-60's jets. Armed with three 2000-lb GBU-31(V)2/Bs, VMFA-115's F/A-18A+ BuNo 163145 taxies over CVN-75's sodden flightdeck on 24 March 2003. Capt Eric Jakubowski dropped his first bombs of the war during this period;

'It was very impressive when all four of us dropped our 12 JDAM simultaneously. I remember looking across the formation and seeing all the bombs falling off of the other three aircraft. Each one guided precisely to its target, which we couldn't actually see' (*US Navy*)

VMFA-115's CAG jet (BuNo 163133) joins the recovery pattern overhead CVN-75 on 8 April 2003 (*Maj Eric Jakubowski*)

breached the berms separating Iraq from Kuwait, VMFA-115 was still unsure as to how it would be employed in OIF, despite having been on-station off the Turkish coast aboard CVN-75 since late December 2002!

Ultimately, the campaign that was fought by the squadron, and Mediterranean-based TACAIR units as a whole, contrasted markedly with the war waged from aircraft carriers sailing in the NAG, as well as by MAG-11 ashore. Although VMFA-115, and the other TACAIR units in both CVW-3 and CVW-8 (the latter aboard USS *Theodore Roosevelt* (CVN-71)), had started the campaign in a similar fashion to its NAG-based brethren by hitting fixed targets as part of 'Shock and Awe', the squadron soon switched to CAS missions for SOF teams in northern Iraq.

Both air wings had originally been tasked with supporting the 4th Infantry Division's invasion of Iraq from Turkey, the US government having planned on committing 65,000 US Army troops, backed by 225 combat aircraft and 65 helicopters, to fighting the war on the northern front. This deployment proved deeply unpopular in Turkey, however, and despite extreme pressure exerted by the Bush administration – and the offer of $30 billion in loans and aid – the Turkish government voted against granting basing rights to US forces on 1 March 2003.

Pentagon war planners hastily shifted the emphasis of the Navy's TACAIR assets in the Mediterranean away from traditional CAS and refocused it on the support of small SOF teams whose job it was to keep the Iraqi Army's IZ Corps occupied while Coalition forces raced for Baghdad from the south. Relying on tactics developed during OEF, when naval aviation had supported SOF squads operating in isolation in the wilds of Afghanistan, Hornet pilots braved AAA and SAMs and endured awful weather conditions to ensure 24-hour CAS support for Coalition forces in OIF.

But all of this looked extremely unlikely when Turkey also refused to allow CTF-60 aircraft to pass through its airspace when heading to and from targets in northern Iraq. Alternative strike routes for the opening 'Shock and Awe' missions assigned to CVN-71 and CVN-75 on the CAOC's ATO were hastily examined, but with Saudi Arabia also closing off its airspace, it appeared as if VMFA-115 and the rest of CTF-60 were going to be forced to watch OIF 'through the fence'. This all changed on 20 March when the Saudi government relented in the face of diplomatic pressure from the Americans and agreed to allow Coalition jets to pass through its airspace. The Saudis would not, however, allow bombing missions to be launched from bases within its borders.

Two days prior to CVW-3 and CVW-8 conducting their first long range 'Shock and Awe' strike missions, both air wings flew their first sorties over Iraq when they carried out DCA patrols near Al Taqaddum air base. Located only 40 miles due west of Baghdad, Al Taqaddum was deemed to be the most likely location from where IrAF interceptors would launch in opposition to the 'Shock and Awe' strikes by the Mediterranean-based air wings on 22 March.

With ONW having officially ended on 17 March in preparation for OIF, these DCA patrols also allowed Coalition forces to keep tabs on IrAF assets, and to prevent the Iraqis from attempting pre-emptive strikes on Kurdish Peshmerga militia forces massing in the extreme north of the country. Supported by 10th Special Forces Group teams and 1000 troops from the US Army's 173rd Airborne Brigade, the Kurdish fighters would prove critical to the successful outcome of the campaign in the north following the removal of the 4th ID from the fight.

Shortly after midnight on 22 March, 19 aircraft (including two from VMFA-115) launched from CVW-3 on CTF-60's first OIF mission. Some 13 TACAIR jets pressed south into Iraq on what proved to be a very long transit – 1400 miles one way – to the target. Having got to the Saudi-Iraqi border, the Hornet and Tomcat crews rendezvoused with USAF tankers and then pressed on to the target – Al Taqaddum air base.

The CVW-3 crews duly did spectacular work hitting their targets with 2000-lb JDAM, all with GPS accuracy, against aim points spread across the large airfield within a matter of seconds. A follow-up daylight strike (CVN-75 was CTF-60's designated day carrier) was also launched at dawn on 22 March, then the 'Shock and Awe' missions flown via Saudi airspace came to an abrupt halt on the morning of 23 March. Thirty-six hours earlier, and just prior to CVW-3 launching its first strike of OIF, Turkish Defence Minister Vecdi Gonul had announced that the airspace over his country would be opened for use by Coalition combat aircraft.

After taking a day to reposition from the Nile Delta to Op Area One, off the coast of Turkey, CTF-60 shifted the focus of its campaign away from fixed infrastructure targets and onto highly flexible CAS operations. Its partners on the ground in northern Iraq were roughly 1000 Coalition SOF troops, bolstered by as many as 10,000 Peshmerga fighters.

Very few pilots had participated in the opening 'Shock and Awe' strikes, but the increased mission tempo that was put in place from 24 March onwards kept all aircrew busy until war's end. VMFA-115's Capt Eric Jakubowski explained to the author how the flying programme worked aboard CVN-75, and recalled some of the missions that he flew;

'CVW-3 split the air wing up into strike planning teams of about ten people each, and they would plan, brief and launch together as one cycle day after day. A typical team consisted of two Tomcats, four or six Hornets, a Prowler and two Vikings. The Tomcats would head straight to eastern Turkey, where they would gas up, but the shorter-ranged Hornets topped off from the duty S-3s overhead the carrier after launching and then pressed out over Turkey. The F/A-18s would schedule their arrival in eastern Iraq to coincide with the F-14s completing their tanker cycle, and they would then replace the Tomcats on the refuelling baskets.

'The F-14 section then pressed into Iraq, followed by the Hornets 15 minutes later. Each section would usually go off and do its own thing, two jets providing the fighter/SEAD DCA, two more working targets in Mosul and a third section possibly heading south to Kirkuk. The strikers staggered their egress off-station too, so as not to max out the tankers during our mid-cycle tanking. After topping off again, each section went back in-country for one more vul period (period of vulnerability), which lasted about an hour. After completion of the second vul, all jets would once again get gas from the tankers, before heading back to the ship.

'Flexibility was the watchword in the north. Once on-station, things never went as they had been briefed on the boat, but they nevertheless seemed to work out for the guys on the ground. Even if we were scheduled as the DCA section, we carried bombs, and I was often called in to drop that ordnance. Typically, a section that had already dropped their bombs would take over our CAP station so we could employ our ordnance.

'We had spent some six to eight hours conducting dedicated mission planning for the first OIF strike, but within hours of arriving in Op Area One this had dramatically changed. As our comfort level in conducting the administrative portions of the sorties increased (how to fly to/from Iraq, where to tank, who to talk to, etc.), the planning was shortened to 30 minutes. That gave us time to read the ATO, figure out our individual tasking and construct new kneeboard cards for reference in-flight.

'Two hours before launching, the strike team crews conducted a quick standard operational procedures brief in the strike lead's ready room, and then each section conducted their own separate section administrative brief. This still allowed enough time to get some chow or go to the bathroom, before getting suited up about an hour prior to launch.

'On the first mission that I actually got to drop bombs, my wingman and I had been pushed up to 35,000 ft by a thick undercast. We were just above the cloud tops, and although we were confident that we were out of the SAM MEZ, we would have liked a little more space between us and the clouds. We each dropped three JDAM on coordinates at Qayyarah West airfield, despite never once being able to see the target. My section was part of a dedicated air wing strike force that dropped a total of 16 JDAM on the airfield, before turning around and heading home.

'About 25 per cent of all the missions that my unit flew in OIF were dedicated strike sorties that had to be pre-planned prior to take-off. These were amongst the shortest trips that I flew, as we would simply launch, tank, head into Iraq and find our target, drop our JDAM onto the coordinates that we had been given back on the ship, turn around and come home. There was no sense in hanging around over enemy territory once you had dropped your bombs. For the remaining 75 per cent of my sorties, I arrived over Iraq with no specific mission tasking. This meant waiting on-station for a call from our AWACS controller with tasking from someone on the ground who needed our bombs.

'A full 25 per cent of the missions I flew in support of FACs saw my section helping to prevent ground forces threatened with being overrun. Another 25 per cent of the missions saw us helping out troops who were being harassed by Iraqi forces, but not threatened with immediate capture. For the remaining 50 per cent of the time it almost felt like the SOF guys were on top of a hill relaxing in a lounger and kicking back a beer, and they just wanted to see something blow up!

'A highlight of OIF for me was performing buddy-lasing with F-14s from VF-32, taking advantage of their jet's superior targeting pod, rather than relying on our less-capable NITE Hawk. The Tomcat crews would drop all of their bombs first and then we would join up on them and they would lase targets for our LGBs. Their greater fuel capacity allowed them to stay on-station for two cycles, lasing targets for four Hornets, before heading back to the tanker for gas. This tactic served us well in CVW-3, as you had aircrew on-station in the area who knew where the targets were, and they could immediately point these out to the newly-arrived Hornet pilots who didn't have nearly the same loiter time available.

'My most memorable mission involving F-14s buddy-lasing took place in early April near Mosul. SOF guys were pinned down along a riverbank by mechanised forces, and we could hear the urgency in their voices in the turnover brief (given by the departing TACAIR section to the controlling agency as they left Iraq), which was passed to us when we checked in. As we headed south, the FAC's calls for help grew more frantic.

'By the time we reached the target area it was sunset, and we could not break out the enemy positions with either our radar or our NITE Hawk pods. We called for the Tomcat section from VF-32 on their tactical frequency and were able to get them to roll from their mission over to us. Within minutes they had located individual revetments housing Iraqi armour and troops, and they quickly provided us with accurate GPS coordinates for our JDAM. We made our first attack with the J-weapons, and then followed this up with two LGB runs that saw bombs guided by the FAC in close contact with the enemy.'

With the fall of Tikrit to the Marine Corps' Task Force *Tripoli* on 15 April, the war ended for CTF-60. On 20 April CVW-3 officially

The CAG jet flies over Qayyarah West air base post-war. Note the darkened patches on the runway, caused by JDAM strikes. This airfield was one of CVW-3's first targets. Although the air wing's oldest Hornets, the F/A-18A+s proved popular with their pilots, as Capt Eric Jakubowski recalls;

'Following the completion of modification Engineering Change Proposal 583, our jets were equivalent in their capabilities to Lot XIX F/A-18Cs in respect to their avionics, but with the lighter weight of the F/A-18A. The old wiring was replaced with digital cables, allowing us to carry J-weapons and AMRAAM. We also gained new radios, a combined interrogator/ transponder and a new radar that had better air and ground resolution and sensitivity.

'The lighter weight of the A+ meant that we could carry two extra bombs in comparison with the Navy C-models in CVW-3. This had little impact at the beginning of the war, when everybody was launching with as many bombs as they could carry and usually dropping all of them. However, towards the end of OIF, when we were struggling to find targets, and you weren't allowed to drop unused ordnance in in order to get down to your landing weight, jets had to be launched with a recoverable load. For the F/A-18C, that meant launching with just one 1000-lb LGB or JDAM – not much "bang for your buck" during a five-hour mission! Thanks to our lighter weight, we could launch with three 1000-lb bombs and bring all of them safely back to the ship if we failed to find a target' (*Maj Eric Jakubowski*)

Tankers were as hard to come by in the north as they were in the south during OIF, and that was not good news if you were flying a typically fuel-critical Hornet somewhere over enemy territory. Sights such as this regularly greeted CTF-60's TACAIR pilots as they rendezvoused with the duty KC-135s or KC-10s manning the three different tanker holding patterns, one of which was over Turkey and the remaining two over Iraq itself (*Maj Eric Jakubowski*)

VMFA-115's CAG jet takes on fuel from a 100th ARW KC-135R over a typically cloudy Iraq on 7 April 2003. Waiting its turn to tank is VF-32's F-14B BuNo 163216 (*Maj Eric Jakubowski*)

completed its OIF campaign, and on this day Capt Jakubowski flew one of his last missions over Iraq. It was a memorable event;

'My section got a call from a Marine patrol in Mosul that had been surrounded by an angry mob in the city itself. The FAC on the spot asked us for our support, but not to drop ordnance or strafe. By then you had to get clearance from the JFACC in order to drop bombs anywhere in Iraq, so the only option left open to us was to get down low and fly a series of fast, noisy passes over the mob at a height of just 300 ft. And that is exactly what we did, hitting 600 knots as we streaked over the city in combat spread at low altitude, engaging full afterburner directly over the crowd. Moments later, a much happier FAC got on the radio and told us that that had done the trick – the Iraqis were fleeing in all directions!'

VMFA-115 had flown 251 sorties (1241 hours) between 20 March and 20 April, dropping more than 300,000 lbs of ordnance. CVN-75 left the Mediterranean on 2 May and headed home. VMFA-115, again embarked in CVN-75, would return to Iraqi skies just 18 months later.

ONGOING OPS

Major hostilities in Iraq were officially declared over by President George W Bush as he stood on the flightdeck of USS *Abraham Lincoln* (CVN-72) on 1 May 2003. However, a steady increase in the wave of terrorist attacks perpetrated by a well-organised army of foreign insurgents, bolstered by Iraqi recruits, has kept Marine Corps Hornets busy across the country since the end of OIF I.

The first unit to experience combat in post-war Iraq was VMFA-312, whose dozen F/A-18A+s arrived in the NAG aboard CVN-65 in October 2003. Assigned to CVW-1, the unit became the air wing's first bomb droppers on 18 November when a section of jets delivered two GBU-35s on a mortar position that had been shelling Coalition troops near Kirkuk. The Ground FAC (GFAC) controlling the strike reported good hits.

CVW-1 was providing TACAIR support for Operation *Iron Hammer* at the time, which was just one in a series of offensives mounted in an attempt to flush out insurgency strongholds in northern Iraq. Several days later two more GBU-35s were dropped by squadron CO, Lt Col 'Giant' Snider, and Maj 'Speedo' Latt on a Fedayeen observation position (OP) that overlooked a main highway north of Baghdad. Previously used to coordinate ambushes on convoys, the OP was gutted by two direct hits.

Both pilots then circled overhead and prepared to conduct another attack, this time with their 500-lb GBU-12 LGBs. However, their GFAC aborted the next pass after an adjacent unit felt that the OP that had been hit was in its sector, and it had been surprised by the JDAM strike! The VMFA-312 jets orbited overhead, waiting patiently for the two units to resolve their cross-boundary coordination issues. The conflict was not resolved before the pilots had to depart for the ship due to bingo fuel.

Aside from very occasionally dropping ordnance in anger, VMFA-312 spent much of its time training with the Joint Tactical Air Controllers (JTACs, as FACs were renamed post-OIF I) in-theatre. The Marine Corps Hornet pilots were pleasantly surprised at the skill levels exhibited

The pilot of VMFA-312's F/A-18A+ BuNo 163169 is given the signal that he is cleared to launch from CVN-65's bow catapult two by the yellow-shirted 'shooter' (catapult officer). The aircraft is carrying an inert Mk 82 500-lb bomb on its starboard outer wing pylon, which suggests that the pilot is heading for the Udairi bombing range on a training mission. This photograph was taken in the NAG on 5 January 2004 (*US Navy*)

by the Army JTACs they worked with, having heard 'horror stories' from OIF I. They found that the biggest doctrinal change from OIF I was the employment of JDAM as a CAS weapon, rather than LGBs. In order to achieve the accuracy required to employ GBU-35s safely in 'danger close' situations in urban areas, Army JTACs, who were not aviators, had to be thoroughly educated about how little battlefield detail an aviator could see from the usual JDAM delivery altitudes of 20,000-30,000 ft.

VMFA-312 also performed countless Route Reconnaissance missions over major roads and pipelines that the insurgents had targeted or could possibly threaten. A staple mission for TACAIR assets in Iraq since OIF I, 'Route Recon' was one area where the aviators of VMFA-312 had an opportunity to instruct their Navy compatriots. Armed Reconnaissance is still an integral part of the Marine Corps Training and Readiness programme for TACAIR crews, so the Marine pilots taught visual reconnaissance techniques (such as how to position a wingman so that your 'look' areas overlapped). Transition Attacks (how to attack a target that is too close for you to roll-in on, without flying out of visual range to set up a dedicated attack) and Reactive Weaponeering (how to maximise the weapon load you are given versus a wide variety of target sets) techniques were also passed on to their Navy counterparts in CVW-1.

MARINE AIR ASHORE

CVN-65 chopped out of Fifth Fleet control in February 2004, and some nine months would pass before the next carrier-based Marine Corps Hornet squadron would arrive in the NAG. By then, Marine Air had established itself in a major way at the ex-IrAF base at Al Asad, 100 miles west of Baghdad. The second-largest airfield in Iraq, with 33 hardened aircraft shelters, 14,000-ft and 13,000-ft runways and a huge bomb dump facility, Al Asad had been home to three IrAF fighter units pre-OIF I. Captured by the Australian SAS right at the end of the war, the base was handed over to I MEF and renamed Forward Operating Base Al Asad.

The base was quickly identified as being the ideal location for aviation elements of the MAGTF that had deployed to Iraq to replace Army units in early 2004. CENTCOM had made I MEF responsible for security in the western half of the country from the centre of Baghdad, while the Army and the Air Force handled anti-insurgent activity in the east.

All land-based Marine Corps aircraft in-theatre are assigned to the 3rd MAW's MAG-16, and in early August 2004 the MAGTF received a huge boost when the 12 F/A-18Ds of VMFA(AW)-242 arrived at Al Asad from their home base at Miramar. The unit began round-the-clock operations almost as soon at it arrived in Iraq, flying its first sorties just 36 hours after landing at Al Asad. VMFA(AW)-242's assignment to MAG-16 signalled the first time that the unit had conducted combat operations in 34 years. Setting the tone for the deployment, the squadron dropped ordnance on several hideouts and mortar positions in I MEF's AOR within 48 hours of declaring itself mission ready.

The 19 pilots, 19 WSOs and 202 Marines and sailors of VMFA(AW)-242 would duly sustain 24-hour flight operations seven days a week without any sustained break for the next seven months. Indeed, the unit had just one full day off and three reduced flying/maintenance days out of the 210 that it was at Al Asad.

VMFA(AW)-242 was well equipped to fly the various missions it was assigned in-theatre, as its jets were modified to carry the new Northrop Grumman Litening II Advanced Targeting (AT) FLIR that had proven so effective in OIF I when carried by Marine Corps AV-8Bs. The unit's Weapons and Tactics Instructor, Maj Marvin Reed, explained;

'Our 12 F/A-18Ds were all Lot XX/XXI airframes, which were the last legacy model jets built prior to production switching to the F/A-18E/F Super Hornet. Having completed our pre-deployment training by late June, we started having a number of our jets modified with systems upgrades prior to heading to Al Asad. We also swapped four of our unmodified jets for upgraded F/A-18Ds from VMFA(AW)-121, the latter being Litening pod-capable.

'The availability of 11 Litening pods in-theatre gave us the greatest boost in terms of operational capability. Two of the pods were also capable of being ISR (intelligence, surveillance, reconnaissance) datalinked with Marine Corps forces on the ground. This meant that aircrew could relay pod-generated imagery that they were looking at on their screens in the cockpit down to datalink-equipped Marines or JTACs actually involved in the convoy protection or firefights at ground level. The JTAC now knew exactly what I was seeing from 10,000-15,000 ft.

'The Litening pod has an excellent field-of-view from the centreline station, which allows us in turn to derive maximum value from its TV and IR sensors. Its picture recording capability is also unmatched, thus expediting the collation of our bomb hit assessment and intelligence reports post-mission. The pod can also laser designate targets for LGBs and LMAVs, as well as being able to laser-track a target that someone else is designating for us. Finally, the Litening has an infrared pointer that,

The 19 pilots, 19 WSOs and 202 Marines and sailors of VMFA(AW)-242 enjoy a brief break from their punishing '24/7' flight operations schedule to pose for a photograph at Al Asad on 23 November 2004. Sat on the cockpit sills of the unit's colour jet are squadron CO Lt Col 'Wolfy' liams (right) and XO Lt Col Doug Pasnik. The maintenance personnel seen here were the unsung heroes of the deployment according to Maj Marvin Reed;

'Thanks to the exceptional maintenance effort by our enlisted Marines, 90 per cent of our aircraft were fully mission-capable for the entire deployment. This meant that we could declare ten or eleven of our twelve aircraft available to the CAOC every single day that we were in Iraq. As an example of what our groundcrew achieved, during the seven months that we were deployed, the maintenance personnel carried out 42 phased airframe inspections and changed 35 engines. At home, a phased inspection would usually take about four days to complete, but whilst at Al Asad our Marines were carrying these out in less than 24 hours' (*Lt Col Doug Pasnik*)

Al Asad is one of the biggest air bases in Iraq, with a perimeter fence that runs for over 23 kilometres. Highly vulnerable to insurgent attacks, the airfield relies on dedicated II MEF security personnel to ensure that the base is protected at all times. These M1A1 Abrams stopped by one of the numerous dispersal areas scattered across Al Asad during a perimeter patrol. The two AV-8B+s parked inside the covered revetment belong to VMA-214. Maj Reed recalled a typical attack on Al Asad during VMFA(AW)-242's time in-theatre;

'During our time in the AOR, the base was regularly attacked by insurgents, who would fire 120 mm mortar shells at us. Although these rarely caused any damage, several did hit one of the three fuel farms at Al Asad whilst we there, starting a huge blaze' (*Capt Matt Merrill*)

Armed with 'Willie-Pete' rocket pods, Litening II (AT) FLIR-equipped F/A-18D BuNo 165410 drops away from the tanker on 3 January 2005 (*Capt Matt Merrill*)

when turned on at night, can be seen by a Marine wearing NVGs. He can then walk my pointer onto the target he wants hit just by him talking to me on the radio. The unit used this method two times in the AOR when Marine squad leaders, operating independently of JFACs, succeeded in telling us exactly what they wanted bombed. In OIF I we lacked such a device in our NITE Hawk pods, which would have meant that such requests would have remained unfulfilled because we needed to have a FAC on hand to ensure that we hit the right target.

'The 11 Litening pods that we had in-theatre were also very reliable, and we suffered only one failure in 8000 combat hours. This was a truly amazing statistic when compared with the serviceability rates that we had experienced with the NITE Hawk pod on past combat deployments.'

VMFA(AW)-242 XO, Lt Col Doug Pasnik, was fulsome in his praise of the Litening pod, explaining to the author;

'The ability of the F/A-18D to carry out offensive air support missions has been exponentially enhanced thanks to the Litening II (AT) FLIR. Now CAS and FAC(A) aircrew routinely augment JFAC situational awareness to a level never before achieved in the low and medium threat environment, introducing an enhanced ISR capability to the battlefield that often allows aircrew to see enemy movement before it can be reported through the chain, or where it could never have been seen before.

'Examples abound where aircrew have traced and foiled Improvised Explosive Device (IED) emplacement operations by insurgents, tracked individual cell movement during Falluja clean-up operations and produced targeting information that allowed "danger close" missions to be conducted with relative ease. The common theme and realisation amongst aircrew is that "we could not perform this mission in the Hornet without the addition of this sensor, for it has revolutionised our awareness and the way we employ precision munitions in this environment".'

Maj Marvin Reed provided details of some of the types of missions flown where the Litening II (AT) FLIR really came into its own;

'My unit conducted plenty of CAS/XCAS and FAC(A) sorties, and our ability to control aviation fires into the battlespaces was particularly highly valued by I MEF, as quite often there was no JFAC on the ground in the AOR to control TACAIR. We were also kept very busy flying convoy escort, counter-indirect fire and counter-IED sorties. These were non-traditional missions that we started training for about a month prior to deploying to Iraq as part of our Exercise *Desert Talon* MAWTS-1 work-up at MCAS Yuma, in Arizona.

'All Marine Hornet squadrons bound for Iraq conduct this work-up training phase on the Yuma ranges, where we also build up our Mission Planning Cell with the help of specialist instructors on base. The month we spent with MAWTS-1 proved to be time well spent, as around 50 per cent of our sorties in-theatre saw us flying non-traditional missions.

'During OIF II, the unit also conducted search and seizure support, armed reconnaissance and precision strikes against known targets. Finally, on-call CAS and manning the Alert 30 and 60 jets were also regular missions conducted by our aircrew, and it was vitally important that we performed the latter sorties as expeditiously as possible, as we were the closest fixed-wing TACAIR assets for our Marines on the ground.

'The squadron was usually called into action when Coalition forces had troops in contact with the insurgents. Typically, these were "danger close" situations, which meant that if we dropped ordnance against the enemy then our bombs might also have an adverse effect on our own forces. A 500-lb LGB or JDAM, for example, has a frag pattern of roughly 900 metres, yet we were being cleared to drop these weapons within 200 metres of friendly troops due to the ferocity of the engagements. If you had told me two years ago that this was how we would be waging war in Iraq in 2004-05, then I would have said that you were crazy. However, with the advent of the Litening II (AT) FLIR pod, our situational awareness and precision has improved dramatically since OIF I – hence our clearance to drop 500-lb bombs in "danger close" situations.'

Convoy protection has been a major mission for every TACAIR unit committed to the Iraqi AOR since OIF I, and this was very much the case for VMFA(AW)-242 too, as Maj Reed explained;

'When fragged to support a convoy from say Kuwait to Baghdad, we would depart Al Asad and head south to pick up the vehicles just prior to them crossing into Iraq. We would establish radio communication with the convoy, and then conduct route-of-march runs ahead of the Coalition vehicles as we escorted them all the way to their final destination. During the time it took the convoy to reach Baghdad, our unit might swap jets two or three times overhead, depending on the progress made by the vehicles and the fuel usage of the aircraft on-station. Being based at Al Asad meant that we could also react quickly to any attacks on a convoy that we weren't initially tasked with supporting.

'By operating in the AOR on a daily basis for months on end, we soon became adept at spotting suspicious activity along the highways and in the cities in Iraq. This allowed us to forewarn the convoy or ground commander of what lay ahead of him well in advance. We scoured the highways for insurgents preparing to ambush the convoy, or setting up roadside IEDs or VBIEDs (Vehicular-Borne Improvised Explosive Devices). In a worst-case scenario, where we were required to act in a reactive capacity once we had identified insurgents on the ground carrying out terrorist activity, we had the capability to hit them hard with clinical accuracy using JDAM, LGBs, LMAVs or 20 mm cannon. If they were too close to friendly forces or non-combatants, and a positive ID could not be made, we would resort to show-of-force, 300-ft low-level, high-speed flybys in an effort to get them to desist in their activities.

'In order to maximise our mission flexibility on these sorties, we had three load-outs that we flew with in the AOR. These usually featured a mix of 500-lb LGBs, JDAM, LMAVs, five-inch unguided rockets and 20 mm cannon. If we were scheduled to operate in Falluja or An`Najaf during the autumn offensives of 2004, we would maximise our precision-guided ordnance load-out by restricting our external fuel to a single tank on the inner port wing pylon. This left the outer port wing pylon free for an LMAV, while the starboard wing pylons would boast two 500-lb LGBs on a dual ejector rack inboard and a 500-lb JDAM outboard.

'On 7 October 2004, VMFA(AW)-242 became the very first Navy or Marine Corps unit to carry and employ the new 500-lb GBU-38 "J-82" JDAM in combat while supporting Operation *Braxton* in northern Falluja. The centreline station was occupied by the Litening pod.

'Although this may not seem like a huge bomb load in terms of tonnage, for Marines on the ground that we were supporting, timeliness, accuracy and precision were more important than quantity.'

PHANTOM FURY

During VMFA(AW)-242's seven months in the AOR, it supported more than 80 named operations as I MEF traded blows with the growing insurgency in the 'Sunni Triangle', as well as northern and western Iraq. Undoubtedly the biggest campaign that the unit participated in was *Phantom Fury*, launched on 8 November 2004, when 10,000 Marines and US Army soldiers, supported by 5000 troops from the Iraqi Army, surrounded the insurgency stronghold of Falluja, just 75 miles east of Al Asad. The city held countless numbers of weapons caches, torture chambers, hundreds of IEDs, booby traps and some 5000 insurgents.

Lt Col Pasnik detailed the crucial role that VMFA(AW)-242 played in the bloody fight for the control of Falluja;

'The unit opened the *Phantom Fury* assault on the morning of 8 November with the delivery of eight 2000-lb GBU-31 JDAM that breached a 50-ft berm north of the city, thus setting in motion the ground assault. The squadron continued with "surge operations" throughout the campaign, completing 1400 combat flight hours in around-the-clock missions, providing an eye in the sky for assaulting forces and expending over 253,000 lbs of ordnance on targets in the city. Some 75 per cent of all our sorties in November were flown directly in support of the Marines on the ground in Falluja, and nearly all of these missions involved CAS conducted under challenging "troops in contact" and "danger close" situations. All were executed without a single fratricidal incident.'

Thanks to Al Asad's close proximity to Falluja, VMFA(AW)-242 crews could drop all of their ordnance, return to base to rearm and refuel and then be back overhead the troops ready to hit more targets in just 45 minutes.

VMFA(AW-242) first tour pilot Capt Matt Merrill provided the author with the following account of one of his more memorable

Phantom Fury missions, which happened to be flown on the 229th birthday of the Marine Corps – 10 November 2004;

'This was an interesting Marine Corps Birthday. After my wingman experienced some trouble and had to return to base, I found myself alone above Falluja at dawn. The insurgents don't like to fight at night due to our advantage with night vision devices, so most of the action occurs during the day. As the sun rose over Baghdad in the east, the Marines on the ground spotted movement towards their positions. For some reason they were unable to get any video or information from the many UAVs circling the city, so my WSO and I were our Marines' only eyes in the sky.

'By this point in the battle the ground forces had already pushed halfway across Falluja. To their south lay the slums of "Queens" and the industrial area of Falluja, known for its large weapons caches and insurgency enclaves. The new day saw many of these insurgents emerge from their hides and begin to head north to attack the Americans.

'Following a great deal of coordination with the units adjacent to his, our 3/5 Battalion Landing Team (BLT) JFAC told us exactly how far south the friendlies went, and where we could and could not fire. With this settled, and groups of insurgents forming in the south, he asked us to strafe down an east-west street to kill or disperse them.

'Our training always tells us to be disciplined with our fires, and to place them on specific aim points, but in this case he wanted "harassing fire" as it's called. I'm never one to argue with a Marine who is being shot at so I of course obliged him. Straight out of your classic World War 2 movie, we put a line of high explosive incendiary 20 mm rounds down an entire city block. As we pulled off-target the road was deserted, the BLT JFAC reporting that our run was effective, and the remaining insurgents had changed their minds about heading toward the Marines of RCT-7.

'Just after our road-clearing exercise, the BLT JFAC began to take well-aimed sniper fire. It became so accurate that he could not raise his head up to look around, but prior to being pinned down he had located the source of the sniper fire as a minaret from a nearby mosque. After going over the necessary political hurdles to have the protected status lifted from the mosque, we were cleared to take out the minaret. We dropped a 500-lb LGB and began to fire our laser at the base of the minaret.

'While a minaret is tall, it is not very wide (four metres at most), so this was going to be a difficult target to hit. The BLT FAC had even approved us to make a second run if our first bomb missed. Steering towards the laser energy we were placing at the base of the minaret, the GBU-12

VMFA-242's colour jet patrols over the suburbs of western Baghdad on 26 January 2005, the aircraft being armed with a single 500-lb GBU-38 JDAM. The unit became quite adept at operating with troops in 'danger close' situations in urban landscapes such as this during the course of its daily sorties in the AOR. This close working relationship with the Marines of I MEF reached its zenith in November 2004 during Operation *Phantom Fury*, which saw Coalition forces make a concerted attempt to rid Falluja of insurgents. Maj Reed explained to the author why the unit had such a bond with the troops on the ground;

'Our ability to perform the CAS mission for our Marines in Falluja was greatly assisted by the fact that we knew many of the JFACs personally who were calling us in for fire support. Indeed, I worked with seven JFACs during the course of *Phantom Fury* that I had either flown with in previous squadron tours or who had served with me in Training Command. There was no other service operating in Iraq that could say that they knew the troops they were dropping their bombs for. Such a close affinity with the JFACs led to some awesome planning capabilities, as we were able to maintain direct e-mail contact with them, or even speak with them over the telephone. This meant that we were constantly updated on their proposed scheme of manoeuvre, allowing us to tailor our mission scheduling and ordnance load-outs to best support their ongoing offensive against the insurgency' (*Capt Matt Merrill*)

VMFA-115 and VF-32 forged a formidable partnership during CVW-3's OIF II deployment in 2004-05, with the pairing of the F-14B 'hunter' and F/A-18A+ 'killer' seeing action during the four months that CVN-75 was in the NAG. VF-32's Lt Cdr Randy Stearns gave the author an overview of how the two units went about their business over Iraq;

'Our missions in-country lasted about 5-6 hours depending on what we were doing. Sometimes guys got extended beyond that. Typically, we would launch from the ship, rendezvous and press out to our first tanker for front side gas. We would then go off and do our mission and hit the mid cycle gas, go back and check-in with the JFAC again and finally hit the back side tanker and then head out of country. VMFA-115 and VF-32 would switch off the lead every other event, and when we got into the target area, the F-14 normally was the one working the LTS pod and talking to the JFAC, since he had the good FLIR for target acquisition. We did a lot of car chasing, building watching during insurgent take-downs and convoy support, along with the usual pipeline patrols.

'In my opinion, the thing that made "Team Vicious" so special was our "can do" attitude and bravado. We happened to be in certain areas where troops were in deep trouble and really counted on air support to make the difference. We didn't hesitate when the call came, and I'm sure that every JFAC in Iraq wanted a "Vicious" section overhead when the shit hit the fan'

ploughed into the dirt just in front of the tower. The LGB penetrated underneath and exploded, sending dust and debris outward in all directions. The Minaret stood for one last second and then collapsed.

'A post-flight review of our video tapes showed that the mosque that stood only a few metres away suffered no damage. More importantly, the Marines could now get out from behind their cover and once again advance to meet the next group of fighters hell bent on killing Americans.

'Now able to survey their surroundings again, the Marines noticed a pick-up truck ferrying fighters between houses and ammunition re-supply points. We circled overhead and followed the truck until it pulled into the carport of a house and began to unload. Shortly thereafter the house received our other 500-lb bomb slamming down through its roof. Now out of ordnance and low on fuel, it was time to return to base.'

Post *Phantom Fury* operations revealed reduced enemy activity in the AOR, and VMFA(AW)-242 transitioned to reconnaissance operations in the area as civilians returned to Falluja. In January 2005 the unit 'surged' again during Operation *Citadel*, providing air support coverage 24 hours a day for a five-day period in support of the Iraqi elections.

By the time the squadron was relieved at Al Asad by a combination of VMFA(AW)-224 and VMFA-142 in January and March 2005, VMFA(AW)-242 had flown 8300 hours in 210 days. The unit averaged close to 1200 flying hours and 550 sorties a month, and no less than 85 per cent of those sorties were flown in direct support of Coalition troops, and in particular I MEF. To put all these figures into perspective, VMFA(AW)-242 would usually fly 4200-4400 hours during a typical year at Miramar. The squadron had flown double this in just seven months in Iraq. It had also expended 408,000 lbs of ordnance, comprising 239 GBU-12s, 64 GBU-38s, 12 GBU-31s, 37 LMAVs and countless 'Willie Pete' five-inch rockets and 20 mm cannon rounds.

VMFA-115 IN THE NAG

On 20 November 2004, VMFA-115 arrived on-station in the NAG aboard CVN-75 to commence operations over Iraq with CVW-3. Capt Chris Holloway, a veteran of OIF I, explains how his unit was employed during its four months with Fifth Fleet in the AOR;

'Within the air wing, VFA-37 and VFA-105 maintained unit section integrity during OIF missions, each pilot flying with a squadronmate. However, VF-32 and VMFA-115 split composition as "Team Vicious" for the entire cruise, each flight (dubbed "Covey") consisting of a single F-14B and a Marine F/A-18A+ sharing leader-wingman roles.

'CVW-3 chose to adopt this composition due to CENTCOM's strict mission requirement for at least one advanced targeting pod per TACAIR section over Iraq. The Tomcat's AN/AAQ-25 LANTIRN Targeting System (LTS), the ASQ-228 ATFLIR and the Litening pod all qualified as 'advanced', but not the AN/AAS-38A NITE Hawk fitted to most legacy Hornets in the fleet. Mixed sections of F-14Bs and F/A-18A+s therefore allowed a more efficient distribution of advanced targeting pods throughout CVW-3, as we only had five ATFLIRs assigned to CVN-75 – we got one pod and the two Navy Hornet units picked up two apiece.

'Although the tempo of combat operations was slower in OIF II than during the war in 2003, the requirement for technical and tactical proficiency was greater. Far fewer weapons were employed (just 20 in total by VMFA-115), but the air wing acquitted itself well whenever the opportunity arose. For example, on the evening of 11 December 2004, a US Army Stryker Brigade was preparing to execute a planned detonation of terrorist weapons found in a sea container on the outskirts of Mosul. A "Team Vicious" section was airborne in the vicinity, and the ground commander advised the flight (call-sign "Vicious 43") that a planned explosion was to occur at a specified time and place. Since nothing else was going on in the immediate area, the two jets flew overhead to watch the detonations, planned to occur near dusk.

'A large explosion lit up the evening sky as scheduled, the weapons cache having been destroyed. Just after the detonation, however, a smaller explosion lit off just south of the troops' position, followed quickly by small arms fire from multiple directions – the Stryker Brigade had been ambushed by a group of insurgent fighters. The JTAC, wounded and pinned down under heavy fire, was unable to control the two jets above.

'The F-14 crew immediately took charge of the situation, assuming the role of a FAC(A) and identifying the friendlies. The crew soon had the hostiles targeted and had provided laser support with their LTS pod for the Marine Hornet's LMAV. The weapon destroyed an insurgent vehicle, after which the pilot pressed home his attack with multiple strafing runs. Low on fuel, he departed for a tanker, leaving the F-14 on-station to provide visual support to the friendlies. The ambush was soon broken.

'As the F/A-18 refuelled from a nearby KC-135, the insurgents massed again for another attack as the wounded soldiers were Medevaced from the ambush zone. The enemy closed on the friendly position, pinning them down with heavy small arms and RPG fire. The F-14, still on-station, targeted the insurgent attack and broke it up with a GBU-12.

'Eighteen days later, in an almost identical operation, a Stryker Brigade convoy conducting cordon and search operation in northwest Mosul came under insurgent attack. A VBIED had been detonated alongside a Stryker vehicle, disabling it. The rest of the unit halted to support the damaged vehicle and had come under fire from insurgents. As the first "Team Vicious" flight arrived on-station overhead, the Hornet pilot in the section spotted a bomb-laden pick-up heading for the exposed troops.

Right
Each toting a single AGM-65E LMAV and a 500-lb GBU-38 JDAM, two F/A-18A+s of VMFA-115 formate with a pair of GBU-12-armed F-14Bs of VF-32 for Erik Hildebrandt's camera. Note that none of the aircraft are armed with air-to-air missiles of any kind. 'Team Vicious' flew numerous 'presence' missions in the weeks leading up to Iraq's national election on 30 January 2005, providing a fair number of the 296 OIF sorties conducted by CVW-3 during 'surge' operations performed between 26 January and 3 February. Usually flying at altitudes above 15,000 ft, the Hornet and Tomcat crews were given permission to descend much lower during the election work-ups and on polling day itself in order to deter insurgent activity and protect election officials transporting ballot boxes. VMFA-115's Capt Chris Holloway recalled;

'There was nothing like being airborne on election day, looking down onto central Baghdad and watching the first free elections take place, knowing full well that you had helped make this historic event happen.'

VF-32's Lt Cdr Dean Castillo also had a great view of the election from the cockpit of his F-14B;

'It was awesome. We called down to the JFACs and they said that everything was going really well on the ground. Flying over polling stations, you could see long lines of Iraqis waiting to cast their votes' (©Erik Hildebrandt/ erik@vulturesrow.com)

'Despite being under "danger close" conditions, the VMFA-115 pilot immediately strafed and exploded the suicide vehicle short of the friendly positions. The insurgents retreated into an abandoned warehouse on the corner of four-way road intersection, where they set up sniper positions and continued to harass the Army troops with small arms and RPG fire. The F-14 crew identified, targeted and designated the hostile building, providing laser support for another LMAV attack, which silenced the enemy fire. The Stryker Brigade was able to egress the area with its damaged vehicle, the insurgent ambush having been broken.'

On 19 March 2005, CVN-75 was relieved in the NAG by CVN-70, embarking CVW-9. Included within the latter air wing was VMFA-323 – undoubtedly Marine Air's most experienced squadron when it comes to operations in the Iraq AOR.

Below
A 'Team Vicious' 'Covey' flight prepares to take on mid cycle gas prior to heading back on patrol. VMFA-115 flew a total of 685 OIF sorties (2566.1 hours) and dropped more than 17,000 lbs of ordnance (20 weapons, consisting of LMAVs, LGBs and JDAM) in anger. This was considerably more than the three Navy TACAIR units assigned to CVW-3 (*VMFA-115*)

AL JABER SWITCH

On 10 January 2005, VMFA(AW)-224's 12 F/A-18Ds arrived at Al Asad from their home base at MCAS Beaufort, South Carolina. Unusually for a land-based Marine Corps TACAIR unit, VMFA(AW)-224 was assigned directly to the CFACC, rather than I MEF, for its first four months in the AOR. This meant that the squadron received its mission tasking from the USAF via the CAOC. This is essentially how a Marine Corps Hornet squadron embarked on an aircraft carrier in the NAG is controlled too. Occa-

sionally VMFA(AW)-242 would also fly CFACC missions above and beyond its I MEF requirements, as Marine Corps TACAIR is tasked with giving up any excess sorties it generates to the CAOC.

VMFA(AW)-224 dropped its first ordnance on 19 January, when it was tasked by the CAOC to conduct a pre-planned JDAM strike on an insurgent torture facility. Two jets launched with three GBU-31s apiece, which was a highly unusual mission load-out for an F/A-18D.

Two months after VMFA(AW)-242 left the AOR in March 2005, VMFA(AW)-224 finally transitioned from CFACC to II MEF control, the latter having replaced I MEF in-theatre at much the same time.

While flying in support of OIF II, VMFA(AW)-224 participated in Operations *River Blitz*, *Matador*, *Raging Bull*, *Barter Town*, *New Market*, *Spear*, *Dagger*, *Sword* and *Scimitar* in support of RCTs 2 and 8, 3rd Battalion, 25th Marine Regiment, the 2nd Brigade Combat Team and numerous other Army and Air Force units. Furthermore, the squadron expended 65,225 lbs of ordnance and flew 2485 sorties and 7036 hours in direct support of Marine Corps, Army and Coalition ground units.

Much of this weaponry was employed during the 24 sorties that VMFA(AW)-224 flew in direct combat support of Operation *Spear*, which saw Marines and Iraqi Army troops battling insurgents in the town of Karabilah, near the Syrian border. ATARS proved a particularly useful asset during this operation, as WSO Capt Matthew Brown explained;

'Our three ATARS jets flew about 20 per cent of our missions overall, being kept busy reconnoitring areas where II MEF and the CFACC suspected insurgent activity was taking place, or where future offensives were scheduled to be undertaken. We produced 2000+ imagery products for the CFACC and II MEF, with some of our best imagery being taken over Karabilah just prior to *Spear*. This helped to confirm insurgent activity in a suspected terrorist camp that was subsequently raided.'

F/A-18Ds, armed with LGBs and LMAVs, attacked enemy positions, destroying multiple targets including mortar positions and a building the insurgents were using as a VBIED-making factory. The majority of targets were buildings confirmed as insurgent strongholds from where ground forces were taking fire. The squadron also flew one strafing run, firing 20 mm rounds from the aircraft's gun.

For much of the unit's time at Al Asad, VMFA(AW)-224 shared the base with reserve-manned VMFA-142, which had deployed with 12 F/A-18A+s from NAS Atlanta, Georgia, in March 2005. The unit made history in the process, as it was the first time in 52 years that a Marine Corps reserve fixed-wing fighter squadron had been sent into combat. VMFA-142 had just three months to get ready for the deployment, but this was easily achieved by its cadre of high-time pilots. Indeed, most of them had served in the unit for the past five to seven years, and they all had at least 2000 flying hours on fast jets in their log books.

VMFA(AW)-224's unique tiger-striped F/A-18D BuNo 164884 sits in its revetment on 19 January 2005, weighed down by three 2000-lb GBU-31(V)2/B JDAM. This rare weapon loadout was used to full effect on this date, as squadron WSO Capt Matthew Brown recalled;

'Our Hornet led a section strike against a confirmed insurgent torture facility. The "weaponeers" at the CAOC came up with the solution to use two 2000-lb JDAM on each aim point in one building and one each in a second building. My unit hadn't expended ordnance in anger since *Desert Storm* (minus a HARM shot in the late 1990s). The squadron was pretty keyed up and the Marines' energy was through the roof. It was amazing to see the looks on their faces, knowing we were all going to do what we had trained so hard to do, and on a target that demanded destruction. It was nearly an all-junior officer strike. We troubleshot the hell out of the JDAM on deck. We launched ten minutes late and made our way to the target area, checked in and were ready to go to work right away. Our first pass was suitcased and we were aborted for Iraqi civilians in the area. We then aborted the second time due to aircrew error. We then switched to manual on the third pass and dropped all three of our JDAM and Dash-2 dropped one of his into the priority building and obliterated it. Dash-2 dropped his remaining two and they guided like champs, but dudded – really no idea why. An F-15E put a GBU-12 into the building later and detonated at least one of the duds' *(Capt Matthew Brown)*

The unit saw action just days after arriving at Al Asad when, on 18 March, a section provided CAS for the 3rd Battalion, 25th Marine Regiment. The reserve infantry battalion was conducting security patrols in the Al Anbar province when it encountered two men armed with automatic rifles who appeared to be digging a hole for an IED. The Marines engaged the insurgents, who fled to an isolated building. After an exchange of small-arms fire, the VMFA-142 jets arrived and eliminated the threat with two GBU-12s.

These types of missions kept VMFA-142 busy throughout its time in the AOR, the unit having flown some 2500+ sorties totalling more than 5000 hours by the time it

returned home in September. The departure of the reservists left VMFA(AW)-332 as the sole Hornet unit at Al Asad, the Beaufort-based squadron having replaced VMFA(AW)-224 in early August.

VMFA(AW)-332 was kept busy supporting anti-insurgency operations primarily in the Al Anbar province of western Iraq. By November 2005, when this book went to press, the unit had flown 1500 flight hours during nearly 650 sorties, and expended 50,000 lbs of ordnance, since arriving at Al Asad.

CARRIER OPS

As previously mentioned, in mid March 2005 VMFA-323 arrived in the Iraq AOR for its sixth spell of combat operations from the NAG in a decade. Having swapped carriers and air wings since OIF I, the unit quickly got into its stride flying 'presence' missions all over Iraq. Tragically for VMFA-323, the first real episode of note during what had been an uneventful cruise up until then was the loss of squadron XO, Maj John C Spahr, and his wingman, Capt Kelly C Hinz, and their aircraft in a mid-air collision over Iraq during bad weather on the night of 2 May. According to squadron pilot, and OIF I veteran, Capt Guy Ravey;

'The weather at the time of the mishap was quite bad. Extremely low visibilities, high winds and isolated thunderstorms, with embedded icing and hail, were present throughout Iraq that evening. Other jets airborne at the time in-theatre were subjected to moderate to severe turbulence and icing, and numerous aircraft diverted to other bases because of "zero-zero" ("zero ceiling, zero visibility") conditions on deck.

'Search and Rescue assets were launched immediately upon notification of the initial mishap, and they were on scene in short order. I tip my hat to the professionalism and courage of the aircrews and troops who risked their lives in helicopters and vehicles operating in the absolute worst of conditions in an attempt to find our pilots.'

VMFA-142's deployment to Al Asad in March 2005 was unique on two accounts. It was the first reserve-manned Marine Corps fighter unit to deploy to a combat zone since 1953, and it has so far been the only single-seat Hornet unit land-based in the AOR. 'Gator 210' (F/A-18A+ BuNo 162409) was photographed on patrol on 13 April 2005, the aircraft armed with a GBU-38 and a GBU-12. Note also the Litening II (AT) FLIR pod on the jet's centreline station. The latter proved a crucial tool for VMFA-142's pilots when conducting 'POO' (point of origin) ops in Iraq – the staple mission for TACAIR assets in-theatre. Watching through the FLIR's infrared sensors from well above 15,000 ft, crews would track the insurgents back to their base of operations and keep tabs on them until a Marine Corps quick reaction force could mount a raid. The view afforded to a Hornet pilot through the Litening pod during 'POO' ops has been likened to the view of a squad commander on the ground peering down a nearby street from the roof of a two-storey building. With the Coalition troops' goal not to kill insurgents wherever possible, but to capture and interrogate them, 'POO' flights have become integral to the way Marine Corps air power has been employed in-theatre since late 2003 (*VMFA-142*)

Less than a week later, on 8 May, Capt Ravey played a major part in one of the few live fire incidents involving CVW-9 TACAIR during its time in the NAG;

'Capt Chris Cannon and I were on a routine patrol over Iraq when we got called to support some Army OH-58s that were being shot up near Samarrah (about 100 miles northeast of Baghdad) along the Tigris River. The Army helicopters attacked the insurgents' vehicle, but they escaped down into a culvert near the riverbank and shot up the OH-58s as they came by. The helicopters called us in, and over the next 90 minutes we proceeded to shoot everything we had (our GBU-12s, my GBU-38, Chris's LMAV and nearly all of our cannon rounds) in a series of strafing runs. We even thought about shooting our AIM-9Xs into the mess, but those have a small warhead and probably wouldn't have done much good.

'It was by far and away the most taxing and intense mission I have done thus far, and the most satisfying, as we were directly assisting our troops. The guys we supported e-mailed the ship hours later thanking us for our help. Unfortunately, one American soldier was killed in the firefight.'

In mid July 2005 CVN-70 was relieved on-station in the NAG by USS *Nimitz* (CVN-68), which had CVW-11 embarked. One of the four F/A-18 units within the air wing was VMFA-232, making its first combat cruise with the Hornet. Like VMFA-323, the squadron performed countless route reconnaissance and Operation *Sea Dragon* maritime surveillance missions (exclusively in mixed sections with F/A-18Fs of VFA-41 due to limited ATFLIR pod availability), but saw little action. Indeed, for the first time since CVW-17 completed its OSW deployment aboard USS *Dwight D Eisenhower* (CVN-69) in December 1998, CVW-11 departed the NAG in late September 2005 without having expended a single piece of ordnance in anger in Iraq. The author, for one, sincerely hopes that this will be the case with future deployments too.

'Snake 201' (BuNo 164721) of VMFA-323 heads into Iraq on 20 March 2005, soon after the unit had arrived in the NAG with CVW-9 aboard CVN-70. This aircraft is equipped with one of just seven ATFLIR pods passed on to CVW-9 when CVW-3 departed the NAG. It was also one of five VMFA-323 jets modified with the Multifunction Information Distribution System which will eventually be installed in all Marine Corps and Navy F/A-18s. VMFA-323's CAG jet in OIF I, BuNo 164721 was written off in a mid-air collision with 'Snake 210' (BuNo 164732) over Iraq on 2 May 2005. Both pilots died in the accident (*Capt Guy Ravey*)

VMFA-232 is the most recent carrier-based Marine Corps Hornet outfit to patrol Iraqi skies, the squadron being assigned to CVW-11 aboard CVN-68. The unit replaced its early-build F/A-18Cs upon its return to Miramar from OIF I with aircraft from VFA-137, the latter unit switching to the F/A-18E in the summer of 2003. However, the Hornet (BuNo 164956) seen in this photograph, taken during a training flight in the NAG in September 2005, was one of three transferred into VMFA-232 from VMFA-314 in late 2004 (*Maj Eric Jakubowski*)

AUSSIE HORNETS

As President George W Bush was at pains to point out both before, during and after OIF I, the forces of the United States of America were part of a 'Coalition of the Willing' opposed to Saddam Hussein's regime in Iraq. The role played by British forces in the war is well known, even to most Americans, but the contribution made by the third Coalition member has not been so well recorded. As in OEF in Afghanistan in 2001, Australia committed both men and material to the fight in Iraq, although this time on a significantly larger scale.

On 1 February 2003, the Australian government announced that it would forward deploy a squadron of F/A-18A, assorted transport and maritime patrol aircraft and helicopters and an Air Forward Command element to the Middle East Area of Operations (MEAO). The latter, according to an Australian Defence Force (ADF) spokesman, would be 'responsible for coordinating air operations with coalition partners, and providing national control of Royal Australian Air Force (RAAF) assets'.

Recently expanded thanks to substantial funding by the US government, Al Udeid air base, in Qatar, was chosen as the primary operating location for the bulk of the RAAF aircraft allocated to the impending campaign, including the 14 Hornets of No 75 Sqn. Home to the USAF's 379th Air Expeditionary Wing, RAF and US Navy assets and CENTCOM HQ, Al Udeid has yet to be officially named by the Australian Department of Defence as its primary operating base in OIF due to political sensitivities involving host nation Qatar.

The pre-positioning of aircraft – codenamed Operation *Bastille* – saw 14 F/A-18A Hornets from No 75 Sqn head for Al Udeid from their base at RAAF Tindal, in the Northern Territory on 13 February 2003. The aircraft routed via Diego Garcia, tanking seven times from a USAF KC-10 (which had itself been topped off by a KC-135) between Tindal and the British Indian Ocean Territory. After spending two nights at the US base on Diego Garcia, the jets completed their flight to Al Udeid, again with a KC-10 as the mother ship, on 16 February.

The deployment of the Hornets to a potential war zone had great significance for the RAAF, as Australian fighter aircraft had not seen

A KC-10A of the 9th Air Refueling Squadron (ARS)/60th Air Refueling Wing (ARW), based at Al Dhafra in the United Arab Emirates, passes fuel to a trio of RAAF Hornets on the eve of OIF. The aircraft closest to the camera was one of four No 3 Sqn jets seconded to No 75 Sqn for *Falconer*, whilst the fighter plugged into the basket is a No 77 Sqn F/A-18A. This unit also provided four of its HUG 2.1 jets to No 75 Sqn. Flt Lt Peter Weekes enjoyed refuelling from the Extender, but was not so complimentary about the USAF's KC-135;

'Tanking was comfortable from the KC-10, as it had a large and forgiving basket. The KC-135, on the other hand, was a nightmare to refuel from. Although it was easy to actually plug into, staying in the basket and getting gas was challenging to say the least. You had about four feet in which to move around before you got sprayed with fuel or fell out of the basket altogether, with no formation cues to use. The basket was made of hard metal, and was attached to the solid boom by about six feet of hose – crazy design. We nicknamed it the "wrecking ball", and one of our pilots trashed a probe soon after we arrived in-theatre' (*Flt Lt Peter Weekes*)

action since June 1960, when No 78 Wing Sabres attacked suspected communist terrorist positions in northern Malaya during the Malayan Emergency. And the last time the RAAF had dropped a bomb in anger was on 30 May 1971, when a No 2 Sqn Canberra B 20 attacked a Viet Cong stronghold in South Vietnam.

The RAAF had had a taste of operating Hornets within a larger US-led force in late 2001 when No 81 Wing sent four F/A-18As to Diego Garcia to provide terminal air defence for the base, which was home to USAF B-52Hs and B-1Bs committed to the bombing campaign in Afghanistan. The Americans were impressed with the professionalism shown by the RAAF contingent, and in No 81 Wing's overall operational proficiency in recent exercises held both in Australia and the USA. It was therefore an obvious choice for the Australian government to make when it decided to send 14 multi-role Hornets to the MEAO instead of the single-mission F-111. With a proliferation of American F/A-18s committed to OIF, the RAAF's Hornets also scored highly in respect to the commonality of ordnance, spare parts and mission capability.

The aircraft sent to Al Udied were all Hornet Upgrade (HUG) 2.1 jets, built between 1986 and 1990 and recently refurbished with APG-73 radar, APX-11 Combined Interrogator Transponders and an ASN-172 Embedded Global Positioning System within their inertial navigation systems. With improved AMRAAM wiring and other avionics upgrades, the RAAF HUG Hornet is the Australian equivalent of the US Navy/Marine Corps' reworked F/A-18A+.

Only aircraft that had recently emerged from a major servicing were sent to Al Udeid, which meant that Hornets had to be obtained from all three frontline units within No 81 Wing – six came from No 75 Sqn and four each from Nos 3 and 77 Sqns. A handful of augmentee pilots were also drafted in from the other frontline Hornet units to help bolster aircrew numbers in No 75 Sqn to 24.

Soon after arriving in-theatre, RAAF pilots flew practice LGB attacks on buildings in the nearby desert, as Flt Lt Peter Weekes explained;

'We were pleased to see how well our targeting pod works with no humidity – we never see low humidity in Australia, except at Tindal during the dry season. The buildings we picked looked just like footage of exploding Iraqi targets that you saw on television in 1991 when viewed through our DDIs.'

The squadron also did a series of tanking evolutions with USAF KC-135s and KC-10s, as well as Marine Corps KC-130s, when travelling further afield to the military training areas in Kuwait. Finally, two separate 4v4 dogfights were flown against Al Udied-based F-16CJs.

Amongst the 24 aircrew in-theatre with No 75 Sqn was Marine Corps/RAAF Hornet exchange pilot Maj Waylan Cain. Serving as the squadron's B Flight Commander, he explained to the author that the unit had tried to get onto CENTCOM's OSW ATO so as to give its pilots exposure to the way the CAOC ran the airspace in southern Iraq;

'During the three weeks before hostilities, No 75 Sqn attempted to get onto the OSW ATO, but permission was repeatedly denied by the Australian higher command in-theatre. Although the Coalition wanted Australians to fly OSW missions, the federal government in Canberra had sent us to the Middle East to support "offensive operations" against

Iraq. In the government's eyes, OSW didn't warrant our participation. As termed by the Commander Australian Forces (COMAUSFOR), that would have been "Mission Creep".'

INTO ACTION

The Coalition launched its first air strikes against military targets across the country on 20 March 2003. The No 75 Sqn Hornets were airborne right from the start of OIF, or Operation *Falconer* as it was codenamed by the ADF once the war had commenced. Typically flying in pairs or as a four-ship formation, the Hornet pilots initially flew DCA sorties for 'high value' force multiplier aircraft such as E-3 Sentry AWACS, RC-135 and E-8C J-STARS strategic reconnaissance platforms and tankers.

Flt Lt Peter Weekes, flying as wingman to Maj Cain, was airborne on the 20th, performing a DCA and TST mission profile. He recalled;

'We took off at 1345 hrs and entered Kuwaiti airspace, where I immediately saw a major flak cloud above us at about 45,000 ft. I subsequently found out that it was the remnants of a Scud missile that had been shot down by a Patriot launched from Kuwait. We arrived in Saudi airspace to find our KC-135 for the first of three tanker brackets. We took the gas, armed our defensive suite prior to crossing the border, then transited 25 minutes north to our CAP. The latter was about 100 nautical miles southeast of Baghdad, near Al Kut and Ad Diwaniyah.

'There were two other Aussie two-ship sections rotating with us between the CAP and the tanker. The radios were a-buzz with calls of new SA-3 and SA-6 sites that had been located, and various authorities for packages to drop ordnance on targets in the area.

'Late in our second Vul, Maj Cain and I (call-signs "Opium 31" and "32") were committed by "Karma" (our AWACS controller) onto a "Bogey" group about 30 nautical miles to the northeast of our position. At the same time, "Monty" and "Burry" (call-signs "Manic 33" and "34") were also committed onto a group a bit further from them to the northwest. Our group was labelled "Spades", so we armed up our missiles – the first time Aussie fighters had been armed in conflict for 43 years.

'Unfortunately, we picked nothing up on our radar, nor visually, and were told to return to CAP with no kills. Shortly after that the radios came alive with calls of more Scud launches, but we didn't get tasked to target them, nor could we see them. "Opium" flight went Bingo on fuel, and we returned to Saudi Arabia to get some gas to make the transit home.'

The unit's CO, Wg Cdr 'Mel' (surname withheld by the ADF for security reasons) gave an insight into these early missions to the Australian press in-theatre soon after the conflict had commenced;

'Pilots were basically given a vulnerability period – a period for which they were responsible to defend Coalition forces, not just in the air. Our job was to defend US aircraft against threats from Iraqi jets, and we undertook the mission for the whole time we were allocated to our sector.

'In many ways, these early missions were really the next step up from the training that all the aircrews and the maintenance and supply people have been exercising for many years. The scale of the conflict here is enormous, however, and that is new to all of us. Having said that, we have nevertheless been able to come across the globe, plug into a major theatre of conflict and be very successful at our mission.'

DCA sorties over southern Iraq typically lasted between five and six hours, and saw the jets refuelling three or four times from Coalition tankers due to the considerable distance from Al Udeid to the Iraqi area of operations. 'We'd fly out of our host nation and then we'd refuel up in the Gulf region around Kuwait', remarked Flt Lt Weekes, who was also involved in the Diego Garcia deployment in 2002. 'You would pretty much cross over into Iraq with full tanks. Although most DCA sorties lasted six hours, some of those I was involved in turned out to be nine-hour marathons. This meant that you were strapped into the jet for up to ten-and-a-half hours from the time you had started up until finally shutting down at mission end. Personally, these sorties were the toughest for me, testing my endurance to the limit. It was like being strapped to a kitchen chair and put in a phone box for ten-and-a-half hours.'

A No 75 Sqn Hornet pilot duels with the 'wrecking ball' attached to a 117th ARW KC-135R on 6 April 2003. The Australian jets were not originally scheduled to refuel from the USAF's Stratotankers, as Maj Waylan Cain recalled;

'The RAAF had not previously used KC-135s, and I talked the XO of No 75 Sqn into getting everybody tanker-qualified on the jet pre-war. He agreed, but informed me that the Aussie ATO writers in the CAOC were going to make sure that No 75 Sqn wasn't fragged for the KC-135 once OIF started. As is turned out, we used KC-135s more than any other "big wing" tankers during the conflict. We only busted two probes during the deployment, and they made great plaques!' (*RAAF*)

Eight AIM-120C-5s are readied for uploading onto No 75 Sqn jets. AMRAAMs made way for LGBs within days of the war commencing (*RAAF*)

Grp Capt William Henman, Officer Commanding the Hornets in the MEAO, told the Australian press how his crews were tasked in OIF;

'All mission planning, execution and debriefing was conducted in accordance with the existing doctrinal USAF ATO cycle that was generated from the CAOC on a daily basis. Australian aircraft were thus tasked just as any other Coalition – US or UK – missions. The RAAF squadron and support elements were essentially "embedded" into the USAF Air Expeditionary Wing organisation at the host third nation base.

'We have obviously benefited from the emphasis the ADF has placed on our ability to work seamlessly in a Coalition during many training exercises. Mission Commander training and proficiency during these exercises has been an important focus of No 81 Wing squadrons, and this proved to be a critical contributor to the successful execution of missions over Iraq by Australian aircrew.'

The effectiveness of the RAAF Hornets in-theatre was further enhanced by the secondment of current No 81 Wing pilots to the CAOC, where they were heavily involved in the development of the ATO and the joint target lists. Thanks to their strategic placement, these individuals were able to exert significant influence on how No 75 Sqn's modest assets were employed throughout the campaign.

MISSION LOAD-OUT

When configured for a DCA/TST mission, the Hornets were typically plumbed with three 1250-litre externals tanks. Wingtip-mounted

AIM-9M Sidewinders, three AIM-120A AMRAAMs and a single 500-lb GBU-12 LGB. Within 48 hours of the conflict commencing, DCA jets were switched to the 'swing mission' fit, trading one or more AMRAAMs for an extra GBU-12 or two larger 2000-lb GBU-10s.

For dedicated strike missions, RAAF Hornets were typically configured with two GBU-10s, three tanks and Sidewinders for self-protection. Later in the war, when the unit switched to the CAS role, the GBU-10s were almost totally replaced by lighter GBU-12s.

The first Hornet strike was flown by a jet in the DCA/TST mission configuration on 21 March, and although few precise details have so far emerged about this event, Flt Lt Weekes told the author, 'The pilot involved was given a TST by his AWACS controller, and he did a great pass, despite the AAA that lit up as he did the push over to attack'. The following day, Maj Cain and Flt Lt Weekes performed one of the first kill box/DCA swing missions flown by No 75 Sqn. The latter recalled;

'We were given a kill box to operate in up on the edge of the Baghdad SuperMEZ. Our AWACS controller told us that Roland SAM systems had been spotted within it, along with 36 S-60 60 mm AAA pieces. This meant that any targets that we were going to attack in the kill box would be well defended. Unfortunately, the weather was socked in, so strikes were unlikely. Maj Cain and I (call-signs "Ethen 33" and "34") decided to take a weather recce up north, and we got to within 40 nautical miles of the centre of Baghdad. The kill box was indeed weathered in.

'As we turned around to come back south, we were shot at by AAA. I could see two grey airbursts just behind and below us, and I gave my section leader a heads-up to this effect. The gunners had the azimuth right, but their height finding was off by about 4000 ft, which was good. We passed the Sitrep to our controller and returned to our CAP.

'Late in our second Vul, we were told that the CAOC's Intelligence section had received information that an IrAF B-6 "Badger" bomber

Armed with two 500-lb GBU-12 LGBs, No 75 Sqn's A21-12 heads for Al Taqaddum air base, west of Baghdad, on 14 April 2003. Flt Lt Peter Weekes participated in this mission, and his diary entry on this date read as follows;

'With my wingman and I operating as "Kong 21" and "22", we departed our base just before dawn for a 5.4-hour morning flight, with the sun coming up as we transited with the tanker from a refuelling track in Saudi Arabia to another in Iraq. We watched a beautiful sunrise over enemy territory! Working pretty much over Al Taqaddum airfield, things were a bit different to four weeks earlier, when the IrAF had MiG-25s manning the alert and flying missions out of here on a daily basis. They were our main worry then – no one is too concerned about them now!'
(Flt Lt Peter Weekes)

No 3 Sqn's A21-52 also carries two GBU-12s, as well as three 1250-litre external tanks. This jet dropped five LGBs in anger *(Flt Lt Peter Weekes)*

was being loaded with chemical weapons and was likely to take-off whilst we were still on-station. Maj Cain's radar was unserviceable, so it looked good for me to get a shot at this guy if he got airborne. We stayed on CAP as long as we could, but eventually had to Bingo out and fly the night transit back to the tanker, and then home – without a "Badger"!'

Assigned to V Corps' ASOC, codenamed 'Warhawk', during this early phase of the campaign, No 75 Sqn was often stymied in its attempts to get target tasking in the first week of the war. Perhaps the most frustrated pilot in the unit at this stage of the campaign was Maj Cain;

'During the unit's DCA/TST phase of OIF, I suggested to my senior officers on at least three occasions that we check out with the DASC before leaving the AOR in case they could use our GBU-12s on targets of opportunity. Ultimately, I was told to "pull my head in" over the issue. It really frustrated me. It was not the CO or XO who denied my request. It was the ADF CAOC representative and the Australian brigadier (COMAUSFOR), who once again thought of it as "Mission Creep"!'

As the ground war intensified, and the potential threat posed by the IrAF failed to materialise, No 75 Sqn reverted almost exclusively to flying KI/CAS missions for Coalition forces advancing into Iraq. It was then that Maj Cain finally got his wish granted to support I MEF;

'After figuring out that "Warhawk" was not a good organisation to work for, the Aussies asked to get into I MEF's AOR and were accepted – as any jet carrying bombs was. This made me happy. I just wish they had listened to me earlier, because this was suggested even before OIF started. We worked in front of the Marine Corps advance all the way to Tikrit.

'The KI/CAS strikes that we flew were all easy, as we did not enter the Baghdad Super MEZ – the Aussies did not trust their EW kit, even though it was the same as that fitted to the Marine Corps and Navy Hornets which operated daily over the Iraqi capital. Furthermore, we were not allowed to conduct urban CAS, again following strict orders from higher headquarters – they believed that the chance for collateral damage was too high.'

The first pre-planned Australian strike sorties were conducted on 23 March, the aircraft being part of a larger Coalition strike package that included USAF fighters and US Navy/Marine Corps EA-6B Prowler electronic warfare aircraft. The KI/CAS missions which followed were flown primarily in southern Iraq, RAAF Hornets bombing a variety of static military targets such as fuel dumps, bunkers and ammunition storage facilities. Elements of the 10th Armoured Division were also attacked during late March, as was a regional intelligence and security headquarters in southern Iraq and the Republican Guard's Medina Division.

One of the last pre-planned fixed target strikes flown by No 75 Sqn was performed on 29 March, when two jets dropped three GBU-10s on

A high-time Hornet pilot, Maj Waylan Cain had completed previous frontline tours in F/A-18Ds with VMFA(AW)-242 and -225 prior to applying for the position in the Marine Corps Exchange Pilot Program. His first choice in the programme was Australia (there are also exchange slots open with the Canadian, Spanish, Finnish and Swiss air forces), and he joined the RAAF in 2001. Upon completing his exchange tour in December 2003, Maj Cain joined F/A-18C-equipped VMFA-212, based at MCAS Iwakuni, in Japan. He is still presently serving with this unit (*RAAF*)

A Hornet is dwarfed by a KC-10A during a refuelling cycle. Australian F/A-18As always flew with three external tanks (*Flt Lt Peter Weekes*)

a Baghdad Division Republican Guard command headquarters. One of the pilots involved in this mission recalled;

'The target building was made up of three wings, which meant three DMPIs, so we planned for an attack, followed by a re-attack dropping one bomb per aircraft on each pass. The ordnance on our jets consisted of two GBU-10s, one AIM-120A and two AIM-9Ms apiece. In to work at 0030 hrs for some planning, with roughly a 0500 hrs take-off, made us pretty tired. The attack was a level lay-down from 22,000-24,000 ft, with our threats being numerous mobile SA-13 "Gopher" SAM launchers and nearby KS-19 100 mm AAA batteries.

'Our attack was planned with an east-northeast run-in for low level wind and collateral damage considerations (there was a mosque southeast of the target), then a northerly turn off-target for a re-attack to the south. Further considerations were avoiding the town of Al Amarah due to tactical SAM threats, and the positioning reference of the Iranian border, which was extremely close.

'The attack didn't run overly smoothly, requiring a further re-attack, but we both "shacked" the target and destroyed the building (mission successful). From my estimates, there would have only been a small portion of the building's northern wall left standing. No AAA or SAM resistance was noted, and the whole place had an eerie feel about it, as it was so quiet and tranquil. My flight lead noted later that he too was waiting for something to happen, as it just didn't feel right being that peaceful, except for us knocking walls out of this building.'

The first 14 days of the conflict saw RAAF Hornets regularly flying 12 sorties per day, and in order to avoid No 75 Sqn pilots suffering undue combat fatigue, they were augmented by extra personnel brought in from Hornet units in Australia. By 3 April, the RAAF jets had completed 130 combat sorties (including 70 strike missions) totalling roughly 700 hours. The sortie rate gradually dropped to between six and ten flights a day from 5 April onwards as US forces moved into Baghdad, leaving the Hornets with fewer targets to strike in southern Iraq.

Seven bomb silhouettes are clearly visible on the nose of No 75 Sqn's A21-23, which also boasts a rare full-colour national marking – the latter has now been totally phased out within the RAAF Hornet force. At least 11 of the 14 *Falconer* F/A-18s were adorned with bomb tallies whilst at Al Udeid, although these eventually disappeared once the jets entered deeper maintenance (*RAAF*)

SOF OPERATIONS

On 12 April No 75 Sqn got to operate with the Australian SAS and the 4th Battalion, Royal Australian Regiment, when its Hornets provided CAS for the capture of the huge IrAF base at Al Asad, 100 miles west of Baghdad. Despite no bombs being dropped, it marked the first time that the RAAF had conducted CAS for Australian ground forces since the Vietnam War. This was one of the SAS's last actions in OIF, and its troops found 51 MiG-21s and MiG-25s, assorted helicopters, AAA pieces and a large ammunition dump within the base perimeter.

This mission was typical of those flown by the unit in the final week of OIF, as Maj Cain explained;

'No 75 Sqn operated closely with SOF teams in western Iraq, which were still "Scud hunting" and mopping up pockets of resistance. We also worked with the Royal Marines and other British forces over Basra on "Seersucker" missile hunts too, as well as flying occasional call-on CAS in Baghdad and surrounding areas. Also of note in this last week was the fact that No 75 Sqn utilised airborne "non-lethal" force multiple times. This usually meant that pilots were instructed to fly high-speed, low altitude fly-overs of enemy positions, or supersonic "booms" in their immediate vicinity. On more than one occasion the sections were debriefed by the supported unit that the resistors had capitulated soon after the fly-over. The ground forces were very grateful at not having to go into the defenders' enclaves and "roust them out".'

Flt Lt Weekes had flown a typical 'Scud hunting' mission on 5 April;

'Tasked with "Scud hunting" in the southeastern sector of Iraq, near Basra, my flight lead and I arrived on task after sunset and began checking some coordinates given to us by AWACS. Our controller had received intelligence from a previous TACAIR flight that they had seen something that looked like a "Scud" launcher – "Silkworm/Seersucker" missiles had been regularly fired at Kuwait from this area throughout the war. My FLIR pod was playing up, so it was up to the CO and another two-ship (initially three jets, as they had a Super Hornet tanker with them, but after tanking he left) of Navy Hornets to reconnoitre the area and hopefully find what was suspected to be a launcher.

'The CO did find a suspected launcher in what looked like a military complex, but we couldn't be sure. In the end, we ran out of fuel before we could PID it and had to leave without dropping. We left the Navy

Australian Prime Minister John Howard and his wife Janette visited No 75 Sqn in-theatre on 3 May 2003 as part of their tour of the MEAO. Pilots were allowed to adorn their flightsuits with rank tabs and unit emblems on the day, but no name tags were permitted, as images from the visit were widely published in the Australian press (*RAAF*)

Australian Minister for Defence Robert Hill (wearing civilian attire in the front row) poses with personnel from No 75 Sqn in the MEAO on 22 April 2003. The unit was still conducting patrols over Iraq at this time, hence the two pilots in the group kitted out in flying gear (*RAAF*)

Hornets on task to continue surveillance of what I suspect was a launcher, as it was situated in a military complex.'

Following the fall of Baghdad on 9 April, No 75 Sqn, along with the rest of the Coalition air power in-theatre, turned its attention on the Baathist stronghold of Tikrit. Four days later, RAAF Hornets bombed parked aircraft, tanks and troop positions around the southern outskirts of Tikrit during CAS missions flown in support of the Marine Corps' Task Force *Tripoli*. All these targets were laser-designated and identified by FACs, these strikes being flown in advance of the Marines' attack on the city. Within minutes of the fast jets clearing the area, American main battle tanks drove into central Tikrit and seized the city following fierce street fighting.

Combat missions gradually tailed off after this, and No 75 Sqn dropped its last bombs on 17 April. The unit flew its final combat mission ten days later, followed by its last training mission in-theatre on 2 May. All 14 aircraft returned to RAAF Tindal 12 days later, followed by the bulk of the 250 ground and support personnel on 15 May.

In its three months of active service in the MEAO, No 75 Sqn had flown 2300 hours during the course of 670 sorties, including 1800 hours on 350 combat missions. A total of 122 LGBs were dropped, and all munitions expended were precision-guided.

Perhaps the final word on No 75 Sqn's *Falconer* deployment should go to the unit's most combat-experienced pilot, Maj Waylan Cain;

'I am very grateful that the Aussies took me to war with them. It was a positive experience, and I was proud to serve with the RAAF in OIF. Its pilots are top notch. I would take every single one of them into the Marine Corps without a second thought. *Semper Fidelis* to No 75 Sqn.'

No 77 Sqn's A21-40 slides in behind a KC-135 while two F/A-18Cs from VFA-27 wait their turn on the tanker. The latter jets were assigned to CVW-5, embarked in USS *Kitty Hawk* (CV-63) in the NAG. RAAF Hornet pilots occasionally worked with their US Navy brethren on 'Scud hunting' sorties in southeastern Iraq, particularly towards the end of the war (*US Navy*)

Three No 75 Sqn jets prepare to leave Al Udeid for the last time on their return journey to Tindal, via Diego Garcia, on 12 May 2003 (*RAAF*)

COLOUR PLATES

1

F/A-18A+ BuNo 163133 of VMFA-115, USS Harry S Truman (CVN-75), Mediterranean Sea, April 2003
This Lot IX aircraft, built in early 1987, saw action in *Desert Storm* with VMFA-451 and was then passed on to VMFA-122 when the unit deactivated in January 1997. It was transferred to VMFA-115 the following year, and has been the unit's CAG jet since its refurbishment as an F/A-18A+ in late 2002.

2

F/A-18A+ BuNo 163155 of VMFA-115, USS Harry S Truman (CVN-75), Mediterranean Sea, April 2003
Also a Lot IX jet built in 1987, this aircraft served with VMFA-122 until 2000, when it moved across the Beaufort flightline to VMFA-115. This Hornet also deployed with the squadron to the NAG in 2004-05, again as 'Silver Eagle 207'.

3

F/A-18A+ BuNo 163133 of VMFA-115, USS Harry S Truman (CVN-75), NAG, December 2004
VMFA-115's CAG jet looked almost identical in appearance in 2004-05, although the tail marking now featured a larger 'Old Glory' and an extra star within the dark blue fin tip band.

4

F/A-18D ATARS BuNo 165529 of VMFA(AW)-121, Al Jaber, Kuwait, April 2003
Amongst the penultimate batch of D-model Hornets built for the Marine Corps, this Lot XXI jet was delivered new to VMFA(AW)-225 in late 1999. One of just 17 ATARS jets in frontline service, the aircraft was transferred to VMFA(AW)-121 in late 2000 and was then passed on to VMFA(AW)-242 following its upgrade to Litening II (AT) pod compatibility in early 2004. This jet was one of three ATARS aircraft deployed to Al Asad with VMFA(AW)-242 between August 2004 and March 2005. On 16 April 2003, BuNo 165529 had become the first Hornet to land in Iraq when it was flown into the air base at An Numaniyah by Maj Jeff Ertwine and his WSO while testing a I MEF-installed TACAN and runway arresting gear.

5

F/A-18A+ BuNo 163097 of VMFA-142, Al Asad, Iraq, April 2005
Delivered to the Marine Corps in December 1986, this Lot IX jet also saw combat in *Desert Storm* with VMFA-451. It remained with the unit until the latter was deactivated in January 1997, whereupon it was transferred to VMFA-122. Later that year BuNo 163097 was issued to reserve-manned VMFA-142, with whom it has served ever since.

6

F/A-18D BuNo 164884 of VMFA(AW)-224, Al Asad, Iraq, January 2005
Built in 1993, this Lot XVI jet was initially delivered to VMFA(AW)-332 and then transferred to VMFA(AW)-533 in 1996. It joined VMFA(AW)-224 the following year, and has worn this distinctive Bengal Tiger-striped scheme for several years. The jet was involved in VMFA(AW)-224's first bomb-dropping mission in Iraq on 19 January 2005.

7

F/A-18D BuNo 164694 of VMFA(AW)-224, Al Asad, Iraq, January 2005
A Lot XV jet delivered new to VMFA(AW)-224 in October 1992, this aircraft was passed on to VMFA(AW)-332 in 1996. It returned to VMFA(AW)-224 in 1998, and has been marked up as the unit CO's aircraft since 1999. Note the jet's 'flaming' external tank!

8

F/A-18D BuNo 165532 of VMFA(AW)-225, Al Jaber, Kuwait, April 2003
This Lot XXI Hornet was delivered new to VMFA(AW)-225 in early 2000, and has been the CO's mount for the past five years.

9

F/A-18D BuNo 165686 of VMFA(AW)-225, Al Jaber, Kuwait, April 2003
The penultimate F/A-18D built for the Marine Corps, this aircraft served exclusively with VMFA(AW)-225 until it was transferred to VMFA(AW)-242 just prior to the latter unit's Al Asad deployment in August 2004. Returning to OIF I, BuNo 165686 was marked up (on its port side only) in a one-off 1st Marine Division-inspired scheme on 16-17 April 2003 at Al Jaber specially for the unit's post-war group photo. It also featured rare mission markings in the form of five 'SAM-busting' symbols below the pilot's cockpit on the left side of the jet – these denoted five successful HARM shots. No other mission markings on any Marine Corps Hornets involved in OIF have so far come to light.

10

F/A-18C BuNo 163481 of VMFA-232, Al Jaber, Kuwait, February 2003
Built in 1988, this Lot X jet was issued new to VFA-83 and saw action in *Desert Storm* with the unit as part of CVW-17 aboard USS *Saratoga* (CV-60). It was transferred to newly-redesignated VFA-115 in early 1997 and eventually joined VMFA-232 in 2002 when the former unit converted to F/A-18Es. Marked up as 'Devil 01', BuNo 163481 played an active part in the squadron's OSW/OIF deployment. It was replaced by a younger Lot XVII jet soon after VMFA-232 returned to Miramar.

11

F/A-18C BuNo 163722 of VMFA-232, Al Jaber, Kuwait, March 2003
This Lot XI jet was delivered new to VMFA-232 in 1989 and saw combat with the unit in *Desert Storm* in 1991. Returning to Iraqi skies 12 years

later, it is depicted here armed with two CBU-99 Rockeyes. As with most VMFA-232 jets transferred out of the unit in mid 2003, this aircraft simply moved down the Miramar ramp to VMFAT-101.

12

F/A-18D BuNo 165410 of VMFA(AW)-242, Al Asad, Iraq, November 2004

Lot XX F/A-18D BuNo 165410 was delivered new to VMFA(AW)-225 in early 1998, and then joined VMFA(AW)-121 in late 2000. A veteran of the latter unit's OEF and OSW/OIF deployments in 2002-03, the jet was one of the first F/A-18Ds to be rewired for Litening II (AT) pod compatibility soon after VMFA(AW)-121 returned to Miramar in May 2003. BuNo 165410 was one of six upgraded Hornets transferred by the 'Green Knights' to VMFA(AW)-242 in the summer of 2004 for the latter unit's Al Asad tour. The aircraft became the 'Bats'' colour jet just prior to the squadron heading to Iraq.

13

F/A-18D ATARS BuNo 165411 of VMFA(AW)-242, Al Asad, Iraq, October 2004

Yet another ex-VMFA(AW)-121 (and VMFA(AW)-225) jet, this aircraft was kept busy performing reconnaissance flights from Al Asad. VMFA(AW)-242's three ATARS jets flew about 20 per cent of the unit's missions overall, reconnoitring areas where I MEF believed that suspicious activity was taking place, or where future offensives against the insurgency were scheduled to occur.

14

F/A-18C BuNo 164871 of VMFA-251, Al Jaber, Kuwait, March 2003

A Lot XVI jet, this Hornet was delivered new to VMFA-251 in late 1993. A veteran of three OSW cruises and a single OEF combat deployment, all with CVW-1, this Hornet still serves with the unit.

15

F/A-18C BuNo 164889 of VMFA-251, Al Jaber, Kuwait, March 2003

Also flown exclusively by VMFA-251 since new, this jet is armed with Mk 77 fire bomb canisters.

16

F/A-18A+ BuNo 163132 of VMFA-312, USS Enterprise (CVN-65), NAG, February 2004

Built in 1987, this Lot IX aircraft was issued new to VMFA-122. In 2002 the unit swapped its A-model jets for VMFA-312's F/A-18Cs, which were deemed unsuitable for carrier landings after three cruises with CVW-3. The older Lot IX jets were upgraded to F/A-18A+ specification and VMFA-312 deployed with them as part of CVW-1 in 2003-04. BuNo 163132 received this one-off 'Fight's On' adversary scheme towards the end of the CVN-65 OIF cruise.

17

F/A-18C BuNo 164721 of VMFA-323, USS Constellation (CV-64), NAG, March 2003

Delivered new to VMFA-323 in early 1993, this Lot

XV Hornet served as the unit's CAG jet until 2004. Sent to Baghdad on the first night of 'Shock and Awe', the aircraft was lost in a mid-air collision (with BuNo 164732) over Iraq on 2 May 2005.

18

F/A-18C BuNo 164873 of VMFA-323, USS Constellation (CV-64), NAG, April 2003

This Lot XVI jet spent the first seven years of its service life with VMFAT-101, training new Hornet pilots for the Marine Corps. It joined VMFA-323 in 2000, and has participated in all three combat cruises undertaken by the squadron since then.

19

F/A-18C BuNo 164730 of VMFA-323, USS Carl Vinson (CVN-70), NAG, May 2005

This aircraft is also another VMFA-323 'old stager', having been with the 'Death Rattlers' since 1993. All ten Hornets embarked in CVN-70 in 2004 featured full-colour tail fin bands.

20

F/A-18D BuNo 164959 of VMFA(AW)-533, Al Jaber, Kuwait, April 2003

Lot XVII jet BuNo 164959 was initially delivered to VMFA(AW)-533 in 1993, and was then passed on to VMFA(A)-224 three years later. It moved to VMFA(AW)-332 in 1999 and joined VMFA(AW)-533 in 2002, becoming the unit's colour jet.

21

F/A-18D ATARS BuNo 164886 of VMFA(AW)-533, Al Jaber, Kuwait, April 2003

Also built in 1993, this aircraft has served solely with the 'Hawks' for the past 12 years.

22

F/A-18A HUG A21-55 of No 3 Sqn (assigned to No 75 Sqn), Al Udeid, Qatar, April 2003

Delivered to the RAAF on 22 March 1990, this jet bore a small motif commemorating the 85th anniversary of No 3 Sqn on its nose – this marking dated back to 2001. A21-55 returned home with an eight-bomb mission tally immediately above the anniversary motif.

23

F/A-18A HUG A21-38 of No 75 Sqn, Al Udeid, Qatar, April 2003

Delivered to the Air Force on 29 October 1988, A21-38 was 'zapped' by the Royal Auxiliary Air Force's No 603 Sqn, which had staff deployed on General Duties to Al Udeid as part of the RAF's Operation Telic commitment.

24

F/A-18A HUG A21-40 of No 77 Sqn (assigned to No 75 Sqn), Al Udeid, Qatar, April 2003

One of four No 77 Sqn jets temporarily assigned to No 75 Sqn, this aircraft was the only one of the quartet to feature the unit's 'Grumpy Monkey' and spine/fin chevrons in traditional Brunswick Green. It ended Falconer with a three-bomb mission tally.

INDEX

References to illustrations are shown in **bold**. Plates are shown with page and caption locators in brackets, with 'insignia' plates having an 'I' prefix.